UNDERSTANDING GLOBAL TRADE

UNDERSTANDING
GLOBAL TRADE

Elhanan Helpman

THE BELKNAP PRESS OF

HARVARD UNIVERSITY PRESS

Cambridge, Massachusetts, and London, England

2011

Copyright © 2011 by the President and Fellows of Harvard College
All rights reserved
Printed in the United States of America

Library of Congress Cataloging-in-Publication Data

Helpman, Elhanan.
  Understanding global trade / Elhanan Helpman.
    p. cm.
  Includes bibliographical references and index.
  ISBN 978-0-674-06078-4 (alk. paper)
    1. International trade. 2. Investments, Foreign. 3. Globalization. I. Title.
  HF1379.H457 2011
  382—dc22

2010046981

To Assaf, Nimrod, and Yaren

Contents

Preface

To understand globalization, one needs first to understand what shapes international trade and the organization of production across national boundaries. However, the scholarly literature on this subject—which has evolved over the last two centuries—is huge, and much of it is too technical for nonexperts to understand. Yet it contains many important insights and results that are of interest to a broad audience, including policy makers, political scientists, other social scientists, and people with no scientific background who follow world affairs. My purpose in writing this book has been to help such individuals develop an understanding of these issues. To achieve this aim, the book is written in plain language with minimum use of technical terms. And when a technical term is used, I explain its meaning.

My hope also is that undergraduate and graduate students of economics and other professional economists will find interest in this treatise, which provides an overview of the profession's thinking on these matters. Our understanding of global trade has improved immensely over the generations, as a result of countless efforts by scholars who used theory and empirical analysis to gain insights into the complex forces that mold foreign trade and foreign direct investment. Because the world economy has been continually changing, economists have had repeatedly to reexamine existing views on these issues, to modify analytical frameworks in view of new empirical findings, and to devise new ways for testing propositions that emerged from theory. This research enterprise has entailed a continuous race between a changing world economy and economists' adaptation of analytical and empirical frameworks to fit the changing circumstances.

To bring the reader up to date on the state of this field as speedily as possible, I focus the discussion of the older literature on themes that are important for understanding current events, and I devote more space to the most recent research. The result is that studies from the recent decade are discussed in more detail. As a result, some knowledgeable readers might feel that certain conclusions from this literature have not yet withstood the test of time and should therefore be downplayed, while other readers may feel that different topics should have been covered in more depth. I can understand why different authors might have made different choices. Nevertheless, while this book reflects my biases, I have made an effort to provide a balanced view of the literature. In other words, this is not an undiscriminating review of the field; it reflects my best judgement of what is important, informative, and (I hope) durable.

I owe a debt of gratitude to a number of people who volunteered (under pressure?) their time to improve this manuscript. In addition to the scholars who generously provided data that are used in the text, and who are explicitly acknowledged in every instance in which their data are used, I received many useful comments from Pol Antràs, Harry Flam, Adam Guren, Oleg Itskhoki, Kevin O'Rourke, Gianmarco Ottaviano, Stephen Redding, and Daniel Trefler. Gene Grossman, my long-time collaborator, provided particularly detailed and helpful comments that greatly improved the manuscript. And I am very grateful to Jane Trahan for editorial assistance; as usual, she saved me from many linguistic embarrassments. Finally, I would like to thank the Canadian Institute for Advanced Research for giving me the opportunity to participate in its programs, and the National Science Foundation for financial support.

1

Introduction

International interdependence is a central feature of the world economy. The economic fortunes of countries are intertwined via trade, foreign direct investment, and financial capital flows. Production networks are spread across countries and continents, making the supply of products in one country highly dependent on economic activities in multiple foreign countries. The global crisis of 2008 illustrates this interdependence in a most vivid way; it led to a decline in the volume of world trade by more than one-quarter, negatively impacting countries whose *financial* systems remained sound. Moreover, the historical record shows that long-distance trade interacted in complex ways with economic development, and that it played a central role in the evolution of the world's economy. It is therefore important to understand what drives foreign trade and how trade affects economic outcomes. Building on a large research literature, this book offers this sort of understanding.

Unlike in the natural sciences, where important research objects do not change much over time, in the social sciences generally and in economics particularly, the objects of research alter and reshape. In this respect, international trade is no exception. When countries and regions transform as a result of economic, technological, political, or institutional change, the nature of foreign trade changes too. Moreover, such changes are not rare in historical perspective, but rather frequent. As a result, the thinking on this subject has been repeatedly adapted to varying circumstances. This motif serves as an organizing principle of this book, which explains the evolution of scholarly research on the structure of world trade from its inception to its present form.

While long-distance trade plays an essential role in modern economies, it was also a salient feature of economic development after the Neolithic Revolution, as hunter-gatherers evolved into sedentary societies that specialized in food crops. The importance of trade further increased with the emergence of cities and early civilizations. Caravans traveled along the Fertile Crescent, trading between Mesopotamia and the Levant, and trading routes expanded over time to distant parts of Asia and Europe. The Roman Empire managed an extensive network of trade, which according to McCormick (2001, p. 778) bound together three continents: Europe, western Asia, and Northern Africa. Large volumes of goods traveled by sea and land, including oil and grain, with much of the trade being subsidized by the Empire. Merchandise moved across Europe primarily on north-south routes, and across the Mediterranean.

The collapse of the western part of the Roman Empire in the fifth century C.E. brought many of these developments to a halt. Ward-Perkins (2005) documents the decline of the standard of living in the Empire's regions. He reports archaeological research showing that the Romans lived in a "sophisticated world, in which a north-Italian peasant of the Roman period might eat off tableware from the area near Naples, store liquids in an amphora from North Africa, and sleep under a tiled roof" (pp. 87–88). Long-distance trade was instrumental in preserving this standard of living, which was not limited to the elite but filtered down to the masses through the availability of high-quality functional products. Ward-Perkins' map in figure 5-4 (2005, p. 98) illustrates the wide distribution, across all of Europe and North Africa, of one type of pottery mass-produced in southern France. According to a long-prevailing view, the collapse of the Roman empire was followed by "dark ages."[1]

McCormick (2001) documents in great detail the evolution of communications and the mobility of people across distant regions. He argues that despite the lack of good data on commerce, these developments—which were particularly pronounced during the Carolingian Empire in the eighth century—point to the presence of extensive long-distance trade. European imports of spices were replaced by imports of exotic medicines and new drugs provided by Arab pharmacology, while silk continued to flow into northwest Europe. "To pay for these imports," McCormick states, "Europe produced a rather narrow range of high-value, low-bulk goods. Some textiles, perhaps, and some tin seem plausible, if barely documented. Fur, probably, and Frankish swords certainly were exported to the Muslim world" (p. 791). But the largest exports around 800 were European slaves, who were in high demand in Spain and in the more advanced economies of Africa and Asia. This trade played a central role in the advance of the European economy.

A matrix of traded products across eight regions circa 1000 is provided by Findlay and O'Rourke (2007, table 2.1).[2] According to these data, for example, western Europe exported swords to eastern Europe and slaves and swords to the Islamic world, while eastern Europe exported slaves, furs, and silver to western Europe and the Islamic world, and furs and swords to Central Asia. The Islamic world exported pepper, spices, textiles, silk, and silver to western Europe, and textiles and silver to eastern Europe. It also exported textiles to Central Asia, and textiles, swords, and horses to Sub-Saharan Africa. As a final illustration, East Asia exported silk to the Islamic world, Central Asia, South Asia, and Southeast Asia; it exported porcelain to the Islamic world and South Asia, tea to Central Asia, and copper to Southeast Asia.

The Middle Ages saw an expansion of trade with the rise of city-states such as Venice and Genoa and the advent of the commercial revolution (see Findlay and O'Rourke, 2007, chapter 3). Although quantitative data are hard to come by, Findlay and O'Rourke (p. 140) report Wake's (1986) findings about the spice trade. Pepper imports increased by a modest 20 percent between 1400 and 1500, while imports of spices other than pepper (e.g., cloves and nutmeg) more than doubled during this period. Venice imported about 60 percent of the pepper at the beginning of the period and less than half of the other spices.

Although there is no doubt that the discovery of America by Christopher Columbus in 1492 and the discovery of the passage to the East Indies via the Cape of Good Hope by Vasco da Gama in 1498 had monumental effects on world history and on long-distance trade, historians dispute the immediate impact of these discoveries. The Iberian states of Portugal, Castile, and Aragon had obviously been affected, and the rest of the world was influenced in the following centuries. But how important were these discoveries for the global integration of markets? Some historians argue that world markets were integrated before the age of discovery, while others argue that integration started in earnest only afterward. Surely, the number of voyages to the Americas and the Indies greatly increased as a result of these discoveries, and so did the tonnage of shipments. Yet O'Rourke and Williamson (2002) show that price convergence across regions—which is an important measure of market integration—did not take place before the nineteenth century.[3]

Findlay and O'Rourke (2007, figure 4.5) present data, based on de Vries (1993), on the number of ships sailing to Asia per decade and the tonnage returned by them to Europe. Panel (a) of their figure is reproduced in Figure 1.1.[4] Evidently, Portugal dominated this route in the sixteenth century, after which the Netherlands took over as leader. Moreover, the number of ships that sailed from Portugal declined over time. Nonetheless, the tonnage they brought back to Portugal during the sixteenth century did not fall, because they became bigger and a larger fraction of the departing ships returned (see Findlay and O'Rourke, 2007, p. 185). Portuguese tonnage of shipments started to decline, however, after the rise of competition from the Netherlands, England, and France.

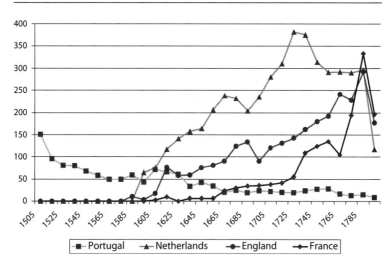

Figure 1.1. Number of ships sailing to Asia per decade. Data from Findlay and O'Rourke (2007, figure 4.5).

Although the discovery of the New World and the passage to the Indies played a prominent role in the evolution of the European economies in the centuries to come, the volume of world trade relative to income remained very small until the nineteenth century, in line with the price convergence argument in O'Rourke and Williamson (2002). According to Estevadeordal, Frantz, and Taylor (2003), imports plus exports reached only 2 percent of gross domestic product (GDP) in 1800, then increased to the first peak of 21 percent in 1913—just prior to World War I—and declined between the two world wars, as shown in Figure 1.2.[5] After World War II trade rose faster than income, as shown in Figure 1.3, and the trade-to-income ratio climbed, surpassing the 1913 peak in the early 1970s. Today the ratio of trade to income is much higher than ever before.

According to O'Rourke and Williamson (2002), long-distance trade in the pre-eighteenth-century period consisted for the most part of non-competing products—that is, products that were not produced in the importing regions (e.g., spices, silk, woolens). In the early nineteenth century

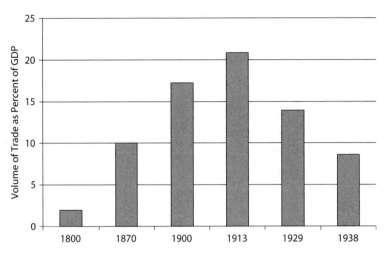

Figure 1.2. World imports plus exports as a percent of world GDP. Data from Estevadeordal, Frantz, and Taylor (2003).

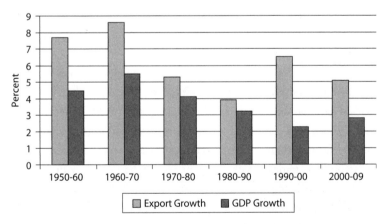

Figure 1.3. Average growth rate per decade of the volume of world exports and GDP. Data from the World Trade Organization, International Trade Statistics, 2009 (accessed online on April 6, 2010).

it also covered significant amounts of basic goods, such as wheat, and simple manufactures, such as textiles. During the nineteenth century, trade expanded rapidly, partly because of an astounding decline in transport costs and partly because of the rise of manufacturing. As a result, price gaps across markets were greatly reduced. The shift from noncompeting to basic goods also enabled trade to expand at a rapid pace. The last phase, which consisted of additional growth and diversification of manufacturing industries and the rise of product differentiation, further enhanced the growth of world trade. That is, the initially low volume of trade and its subsequent growth were materially influenced by the transformation of production and consumption.

While the evolution of long-distance trade was related to economic development, the interdependence between them was complex. In particular, one cannot argue that the effects were unidirectional (i.e., that economic development brought about trade expansion), because long-distance trade affected economic development and economic development affected trade. Moreover, the influence of trade on economic development operated through multiple channels, including institutional and political means.

Long-distance trade in the aftermath of the discovery of the Americas is often cited as a major event that contributed to the divergence in economic conditions between Europe and China. Although Europe and China were similarly advanced in the mid-eighteenth century, the Industrial Revolution took place in Europe, as a result of which Europe grew faster than China. This eventually led to large gaps in income per capita (see Pomeranz, 2000). Naturally, the Industrial Revolution was not driven by trade per se; trade was, rather, a contributing factor. According to Allen (2009), the availability of cheap coal and high wages in England induced the development of technologies that substituted machines for labor, and these technologies fueled British economic growth.[6] As the new technologies spread to continental Europe, they prompted economic growth in the Netherlands first and then in other western European countries.

Acemoglu, Johnson, and Robinson (2005) point out that European growth in the post-1500 period was concentrated in countries with access to the Atlantic Ocean: Britain, France, the Netherlands, Portugal, and Spain, countries that engaged in trade with the New World and acquired overseas colonies. These commercial opportunities strengthened the political power of merchant groups and entrepreneurs and weakened the power of monarchs. As a result, constraints on the executive were broadened and property rights became more secure for a larger segment of society. These unintended consequences of trade with the New World enabled the Atlantic traders to forge ahead of other European countries.[7]

Yet trade with the New World also had negative effects in Spain, where Castilian institutions proved to be inadequate in limiting the power of Philip II. The flow of silver from the Americas encouraged Philip II to engage in wars that eventually became too expensive and required domestic taxes and large loans from foreign bankers. According to Drelichman (2005) and Drelichman and Voth (2008), the ensuing struggles between the Crown and the Cortes weakened domestic institutions, and this had unfortunate consequences for Spanish economic growth.[8]

Although long-distance and international trade are not exactly the same phenomena, they are closely related in that much of long-distance trade is also international trade. True, trade between California and Massachusetts (two states of the United States) is long-distance, as is trade between British Columbia and Quebec (two provinces of Canada), yet neither is international. And trade between Turkey and Syria or Israel and Jordan, which is international, is short-distance in comparison. Nevertheless, our discussion will focus on international trade, emphasizing the movement of products across national borders.

Countries differ in national features that shape the structure of foreign trade, while geographic attributes are more important in shaping trade flows across regions within a country. Moreover, regions within a country are more integrated than regions of different countries. Nevertheless, the fields of international trade and regional economics share common traits that were emphasized already by Ohlin (1933), such as transport costs, agglomeration of economic activity, and the unlinking of production from consumption. My exposition follows the historical evolution of the field of international trade, highlighting the interplay between theory and evidence. In particular, I explain theoretical arguments in the context in which they were developed, the evidence that was amassed to test or challenge them, and modifications of the theoretical arguments that were developed in order to accommodate new evidence. This chain of theorizing, empirical investigation that confirms parts of the theory and contradicts others, and updating of the theory in view of new evidence has been a fruitful pattern in understanding international trade. Moreover, this pattern has been unavoidable in view of the changing nature of international economic interactions. In other words, theories that had been suitable at one time became less appropriate as national economies—and with them patterns of international specialization—changed.

Chapter 2 discusses the two major paradigms of foreign trade that were developed in the early parts of the nineteenth and twentieth centuries, respectively—the former by David Ricardo, the latter by Eli Heckscher and Bertil Ohlin. Each one was cultivated in the context of its time; the former explained trade flows by differences in labor productivity across countries, while the latter explained foreign trade by differences in factor endowments (i.e., the availability of productive resources such as labor, capital, and land). In each case the underlying causes of trade were designed to address specific issues. These two paradigms were extensively studied during most of the twentieth century, and they were applied to a host of issues, such as gains from trade, the conflict of interest between different groups in society concerning the desirability of open markets, the impact of trade policies—including free trade agreements and multilateral trade negotiations—and the relationship between international trade and economic growth. Gains from trade and distributional conflicts are examined in Chapter 3. The impact of trade policies on national economies is a large subject that deserves a book-length treatment of its own, and I have chosen not to cover it in this deliberately short presentation. The relationship between trade and growth is an important subject that is dealt with in detail in Helpman (2004, chapter 5), and since I believe that there is not much new that can be added to that treatment, I have not included it in this book.

While the neoclassical trade theory that dominated the thinking about foreign trade during most of the twentieth century has many merits, it proved inadequate in addressing a number of phenomena that became particularly salient in the post–World War II period. This led to the first major revolution in trade theory—in the early 1980s—and to the development of what was then dubbed the "new" trade theory, which I discuss in Chapter 4. The motivation for this revolution was empirical, and the "new" trade models—which emphasize economies of scale and monopolistic competition—triggered new empirical work. Yet as the nature of world trade kept changing and new data sets became available in the 1990s, the inadequacy of the theoretical models from the 1980s became visible. As a result, a second revolution took place in the early 2000s, this time focusing on characteristics of individual firms and how they engage in international transactions. The first stage of this revolution is discussed in Chapter 5, focusing on trade in goods. The second stage is discussed in Chapter 6, focusing on foreign direct investment (i.e., the ownership of subsidiaries in foreign lands), offshoring, and outsourcing.

One may wonder why foreign direct investment (FDI) has not been mentioned so far. Was it not important in the more distant past and became important only in the 1990s? The answer is, of course, that international capital flows, including FDI, played a major role in economic history, and especially so with the expansion of colonies after the discovery of the New World. Foreign asset holdings, in the form of FDI and foreign financial assets, grew fast in the nineteenth century in tandem with the growth of trade, and their size relative to GDP expanded at the end of the nineteenth century. Though foreign asset holdings collapsed after World War I, like foreign trade, they expanded rapidly again after World War II (see Obstfeld and Taylor, 2004, table 2.1).

Much of the expansion of foreign asset holdings in the postwar period has been portfolio investment, with which we shall not deal in this book. The discussion of FDI, which is intimately related to foreign trade, is relegated to Chapter 6, where it is possible to build on the knowledge acquired in the previous chapters. FDI flows grew fast after World War II, reaching a peak before the collapse of the dotcom bubble in 2001, when they also collapsed. They recovered, regaining their 2001 peak between 2006 and 2007 (see UNCTAD, 2009). Importantly, the emergence of worldwide networks of production, in which multinational corporations play center stage, can be understood only within the broader frameworks discussed in Chapters 4 and 5.

The last chapter provides a brief discussion of two ongoing research programs that are not treated in the main chapters of this book, along with reflections on future directions. Since the study of international trade and foreign direct investment has become highly specialized, I very much hope that this nontechnical exposition of what is known on this subject will help the reader better understand the world around us.

2

Comparative Advantage

Countries have traded with each other since ancient times. King Solomon ordered cedar of Lebanon from King Hiram of Tyre for the construction of the temple in Jerusalem about 3000 years ago (see 1 Kings 5:9), while many residents of modern Jerusalem build their floors from Italian tiles.

Economists have long pondered the question "What drives international trade?" As for cedar of Lebanon, the answer may appear simple: if one insists on building a temple or a palace in Jerusalem from this high-quality aromatic timber, the wood has to be imported from Lebanon, because this is where it grows. And similarly, if one insists on building floors in Jerusalem from Italian tiles, one has to import them from Italy. Yet these answers are not entirely satisfactory. Granted, cedar of Lebanon grows in Lebanon, because the natural conditions of the area support the growth of these trees, and therefore those who wish to use them have to bring them from Lebanon. But why would one insist on using cedar of Lebanon rather than some other timber? Presumably, because the relative cost of good substitutes is not low enough. But if so, why?

The case of Italian tiles is even more difficult, because these tiles, which are made from Italian stone, can be manufactured in Jerusalem; one could import the stone and cut the tiles in the importing country. What is, therefore, so special about the Italian-made tiles that justifies the purchase of tiles from Italy rather than just the stone? And in this case one can also ask "Why use Italian tiles rather than tiles manufactured in another country, such as Turkey, or tiles made from local stones?"

These questions have, of course, no single answer; rather, there are multiple reasons for international trade. Many of the answers are related to forces that shape specialization patterns: differences across countries in technologies, endowments, preferences, institutions, or market structures, to name a few. Adam Smith, for one, noted more than 200 years ago in *The Wealth of Nations* (published in 1776) an analogy between specialization within countries and specialization across them:

> It is the maxim of every prudent master of a family, never to attempt to make at home what it will cost him more to make than to buy. The taylor does not attempt to make his own shoes, but buys them of the shoemaker. The shoemaker does not attempt to make his own clothes, but employs a taylor. The farmer attempts to make neither the one nor the other, but employs those different artificers. All of them find it for their interest to employ their whole industry in a way in which they have some advantage over their neighbours, and to purchase with a part of its produce, or what is the same thing, with the price of a part of it, whatever else they have occasion for.
>
> What is prudence in the conduct of every private family, can scarce be folly in that of a great kingdom. If a foreign country can supply us with a commodity cheaper than we ourselves can make it, better buy it of them with some part of the produce of our own industry, employed in a way in which we have some advantage. (Smith, 1937, p. 424)

Yet this analogy is not entirely satisfactory. First, specialization at the level of a worker or artisan can be easily replicated in different countries. Does the existence of tailors in Italy make unprofitable or undesirable the sewing of garments in France or Germany? If it did, Italy would supply all the apparel worn by Frenchmen and Germans. This conclusion differs greatly from reality, in which many a product is manufactured by a large number of countries. Specialization is hardly *complete*; even if a country excels in the manufacturing of certain goods, it is unlikely to become the sole producer of such goods. Second, what allows a foreign country to "supply us with a commodity cheaper than we ourselves can make it?" Some countries have natural advantages in particular products, such as Lebanon had in cedar wood or Italy has in tiles, and it may be very costly for other countries to manufacture these products. As Adam Smith noted:

> The natural advantages which one country has over another in producing particular commodities are sometimes so great, that it is acknowledged by all the world to be in vain to struggle with them. By means of glasses, hotbeds, and hotwalls, very good grapes can be raised in Scotland, and very good wine too can be made of them at about thirty times the expence for which at least equally good can be brought from foreign countries. Would it be a reasonable law to prohibit the importation of all foreign wines, merely to encourage the making of claret and burgundy in Scotland? But if there would be a manifest absurdity in turning towards any employment, thirty times more of the capital and industry of the country, than would be necessary to purchase from foreign countries an equal quantity of the commodities wanted, there must be an absurdity, though not altogether so glaring, yet exactly of the same kind, in turning towards any such employment a thirtieth, or even a three hundredth part more of either. (Smith, 1937, p. 425)

That is, it does not pay to make products in one country that use resources in excess of the resources needed to acquire the same goods from a foreign country. But then a new question arises: What determines the relative cost of these alternative supply channels: domestic versus foreign? Such relative costs are not God-given, at least not for most products, and they depend on more than what happens in the particular product market. As a rule, they also depend on what happens in other product markets, in labor markets, in markets for machines and equipment, and the like, because costs of production depend on the available technology, the availability of various inputs, and the demand for these inputs from all sources. In other words, relative costs are determined in what economists call "general equilibrium," through the interaction of many sectors and different types of markets. Interdependencies of this kind make the study of international trade and foreign direct investment challenging.

Traditional explanations of comparative advantage focus on *sectoral* trade patterns and emphasize the forces that determine sectoral supplies, where a sector is made up of similar products such as cars or apparel. Trade flows between countries certainly depend on the characteristics of supply systems, but not only on them. A country's trade is determined by the difference between its sectoral supply and demand levels. A country that grows more wheat than it consumes exports wheat, while a country that grows less wheat than it consumes imports wheat. For this reason, forces that shape demand patterns also shape the structure of foreign trade.

The role of demand considerations has been deemphasized, however, first by David Ricardo, the founder of the technological theory of comparative advantage, and subsequently by Eli Heckscher and Bertil Ohlin, the founders of the factor proportions theory of comparative advantage.

2.1 Technology

David Ricardo developed the first comprehensive theory of comparative advantage in chapter 7 of his *On the Principles of Political Economy, and Taxation* (published in 1817). In the same chapter he clarifies what makes differences between countries distinct from differences between regions of the same country, as far as economic activity is concerned. Should the rate of profit on physical capital employed in Yorkshire exceed the rate of profit on physical capital employed in London, capital would speedily move from London to Yorkshire. Similarly with labor, should the real wage rate in one region of a country exceed the real wage rate in another region, workers from the latter region would seek employment in the former. But people and physical capital do not move so swiftly from one country to another. As a result, prices of factor inputs employed in production, which cannot differ much across regions of the same country, can and do differ substantially across countries. This premise is central to Ricardo's view of comparative advantage, and it has been adopted by generations of scholars ever since.

Consider Ricardo's example of trade in wine and cloth between England and Portugal, which is based on his labor theory of value, a theory in which the relative value of goods is determined by the relative amounts of labor embodied in their production. Starting with Portugal, he notes that its rate of exchange with England of wine for cloth is not determined by "the respective quantities of labour devoted to the production of each, as it would be, if both commodities were manufactured in England, or both in Portugal" (Ricardo, 1971, p. 153). In other words, what determines relative prices within a country does not determine them in trading relationships. And he elaborates:

> England may be so circumstanced, that to produce the cloth may require the labour of 100 men for one year; and if she attempted to make the wine, it might require the labour of 120 men for the same time. England would therefore find it her interest to import wine, and to purchase it by the exportation of cloth.
>
> To produce the wine in Portugal, might require only the labour of 80 men for one year, and to produce the cloth in the same country, might require the labour of 90 men for the same time. It would therefore be advantageous for her to export wine in exchange for cloth. This exchange might even take place, notwithstanding that the commodity imported by Portugal could be produced there with less labour than in England. Though she could make the cloth with the labour of 90 men, she would import it from a country where it required the labour of 100 men to produce it, because it would be advantageous to her rather to employ her capital in the production of wine, for which she would obtain more cloth from England, than she could produce by diverting a portion of her capital from the cultivation of vines to the manufacture of cloth.

Thus England would give the produce of the labour of 100 men, for the produce of the labour of 80. Such an exchange could not take place between the individuals of the same country. The labour of 100 Englishmen cannot be given for that of 80 Englishmen, but the produce of the labour of 100 Englishmen may be given for the produce of the labour of 80 Portuguese, 60 Russians, or 120 East Indians. The difference in this respect, between a single country and many, is easily accounted for, by considering the difficulty with which capital moves from one country to another, to seek a more profitable employment, and the activity with which it invariably passes from one province to another in the same country. (Ricardo, 1971, pp. 153–154)

Ricardo then notes that under these circumstances it would be advantageous to move to Portugal the resources that England employs in the production of cloth in order to manufacture cloth in the more efficient country (i.e., the country with the *absolute* advantage in the manufacturing of cloth). But given the attachment of resources to countries, these efficiency gains cannot be realized.

This discussion contains one of the most celebrated results in economics: patterns of specialization and trade are determined by *comparative* advantage and not by *absolute* advantage.[9] England exports cloth despite the fact that it takes more English workers than Portuguese workers to produce the same amount of cloth, because in England the use of labor in the production of cloth relative to the use of labor in the production of wine is 100/120 while in Portugal it is 90/80, and 90/80 is larger than 100/120. In other words, English workers are relatively more efficient in the production of cloth, while Portuguese workers are relatively more efficient in the production of wine. How does this technological data impact wages in the two countries? The wage of Portuguese workers has to be somewhere between 100/90 and 120/80 times the wage of English workers because if it were higher it would be cheaper to manufacture both cloth and wine in England, and if it were lower it would be cheaper to manufacture both cloth and wine in Portugal. In either case there would be no demand for labor in one of the countries, which would drive down that country's wage rate.[10] Where exactly the relative wage settles, and therefore where exactly the price of cloth relative to the price of wine settles, depends on demand conditions.[11] A relatively high demand for cloth would push the relative wage of Portuguese workers closer to 100/90, while a relatively high demand for wine would push it closer to 120/80. Nevertheless, and independently of the resulting relative wage, England exports cloth while Portugal exports wine. Ricardo's system predicts the *direction* of trade flows, a qualitative result, but not the volume of trade. Knowing the technological characteristics of England and Portugal is not enough to predict trade volumes; we also need to know their preferences for cloth and wine.[12]

How widely do Ricardo's insights apply? The answer depends on what one considers to be the core of his argument. If one takes the core to be that differences across countries in sectoral productivity levels are important determinants of international trade flows, and that *relative* productivities are a major source of comparative advantage, then his insights are very general. If, on the other hand, one takes the core of the argument to be a precise prediction of the direction of trade flows, then Ricardo's insights are not very general, because in a complex world with many products and many countries, his type of comparative cost analysis is insufficient for this purpose.

To understand these statements, imagine a world of many countries and many products in which all products are final consumer goods.[13] Every country has its own technology for manufacturing products with labor services, and no other inputs are needed for this purpose. Moreover, every product requires a fixed amount of labor per unit output, independently of the output level. As in Ricardo's example, the relative labor requirements differ across countries and workers do not migrate to other countries.

If we knew the wage rates in all the countries, we could use the information on labor requirements to calculate the cost of producing each product in every country by multiplying the country's wage rate with the product's labor requirement per unit output. Then we could compare these unit costs across countries. In this way we would be able to identify the least-cost country for every product. If the least-cost country for a product, say cloth, happens to be unique, then this country, say England, has to be the sole producer of cloth, which implies that England exports cloth to every other country in the world that wishes to consume cloth.[14] And if the least-cost producer happens to be unique in every industry, then this reasoning identifies the least-cost country of every product as the product's single exporter. In Ricardo's example England is the least-cost manufacturer of cloth and therefore it exports cloth, while Portugal is the least-cost manufacturer of wine and therefore it exports wine.

Two questions emerge from this reasoning. First, what happens when there is more than one least-cost country for some products? Second, what determines the wage rates, and in particular, are the wage rates independent of the patterns of specialization?

Consider, first, multiple countries with the same lowest unit cost. For concreteness, suppose that Portugal and France have the same unit cost for wine, and that all other countries have higher unit costs.[15] Then we can predict that all countries other than Portugal and France import wine and that either Portugal or France or both export wine. That is, both Portugal and France may export wine, France may export wine while Portugal imports wine, or France may import wine while Portugal exports it. To determine the Portuguese and French direction of trade, we need additional information on wine production and consumption. If, for example, Portugal is a least-cost manufacturer of wine only, then Portugal has to export wine in order to pay for its imports of other goods, which it does not produce.[16] But if Portugal is a least-cost producer of various goods in addition to wine, then we need to know how much wine it produces and how much wine it consumes in order to calculate the difference between its wine production and consumption. If production exceeds consumption, Portugal exports wine, but if consumption exceeds production, it imports wine. Evidently, the presence of more than one least-cost country introduces ambiguity into the prediction of trade flows based on purely Ricardian considerations. These ambiguities can be resolved only with the help of additional information on production and consumption.

Next, consider the relationship between wages and patterns of specialization, assuming for simplicity that there are only two countries, England and Portugal, each with only four industries. Figure 2.1 depicts relative labor requirements. In this example it takes 50 percent more labor in England than in Portugal to manufacture cloth, and it takes four times more labor in England than in Portugal to manufacture wine. Between these extremes there are two additional sectors, wood and leather products; England needs twice as many workers than Portugal to manufacture wood products and 2.5 times as many workers to manufacture leather products. In the figure the sectors are arranged according to the order in which England's relative labor requirement rises.

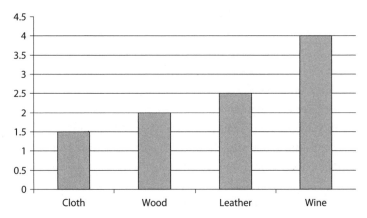

Figure 2.1. Relative labor requirements in four industries.

As in Ricardo's example, here too Portugal is the more efficient economy. As a result, its wage rate has to be higher than the English wage rate. In particular, it has to be between 1.5 times and four times higher, because if the Portuguese wage were higher by less than 50 percent it would be cheaper to manufacture all products in Portugal, and if the Portuguese wage were more than four times higher it would be cheaper to manufacture all products in England. Next, note that if the Portuguese wage were higher by more than 50 percent but less than 100 percent, England would be the least-cost producer of cloth and Portugal would be the least-cost producer of wood products, leather products, and wine. Under the circumstances the world demand for cloth would be siphoned to England and the world demand for the other products would be siphoned to Portugal. To satisfy these demands England would need to employ a certain amount of labor in the production of cloth while Portugal would need to employ a certain amount of labor in the production of the other products. It may then happen that the required labor to manufacture the demanded cloth falls short of England's labor force while the required labor to manufacture the other products exceeds Portugal's labor force.[17] In this event the Portuguese relative wage would be too low.

By similar reasoning we conclude that if the Portuguese wage were to rise so as to be more than twice as high as the English wage but less than 2.5 times higher, England would be the least-cost producer of cloth and wood products and Portugal would be the least-cost producer of leather products and wine. As a result, the world's demand for cloth and wood products would generate labor demand in England while the world's demand for leather products and wine would generate labor demand in Portugal. Then there might exist a relative wage in this range at which the demand for English labor would equal its supply and the demand for Portuguese labor would equal its supply, where the demand for a country's labor is the amount of labor needed by its manufacturers to produce the goods demanded. If this were not the case, and we still found that at all the relative wages in this range labor demand in England fell short of the supply and labor demand in Portugal exceeded the supply, we would conclude that the Portuguese relative wage had to be higher. In particular, we would conclude that the Portuguese wage had to be at least 2.5 times as high as the English wage, but lower than four times the English wage, in which case England would be the least-cost producer of cloth, wood, and leather products, and Portugal would be the least-cost producer of wine only.

What this example illustrates is that wages cannot be determined independently of patterns of specialization; which country produces which products is determined jointly with the wage structure, and the outcome depends on demand conditions, as Mill (1909) noted, as well as on the amounts of labor available in every country.

Dornbusch, Fischer, and Samuelson (1977) developed an elegant framework for studying trade between two countries that have the technical know-how to manufacture a large number of products. They showed how relative wages are determined jointly with patterns of specialization when expenditure shares are the same in every country and they are independent of prices and income (i.e., if people in one country spend one-third of their income on clothing, so do people in every other country, and similarly for food, cars, and all other products).[18] To find relative wages, one starts by ordering relative labor requirements in ascending order for one of the countries, similar to the order depicted in Figure 2.1, but allowing for many products. For every relative wage it is then possible to identify the products that England produces at lower cost and products that Portugal produces at lower cost. With very many products it may happen that a negligible number can be produced in both countries with equal cost, and these can be disregarded. Then one can compute the labor demand in England from the worldwide expenditure on the products for which England is the least-cost manufacturer and the labor demand in Portugal from the worldwide expenditure on the products for which Portugal is the least-cost manufacturer. If these labor demands equal their supplies, we have an equilibrium relative wage. Alternatively, if the labor demand in England exceeds its supply, wages in England must rise relative to those in Portugal for markets to clear. And if labor demand in England falls short of its supply, wages in England must fall relative to those in Portugal for markets to clear. In either case, we know in which direction relative wages adjust. Following this procedure, we find the unique relative wage that equates labor demand with labor supply in each country.

As is evident from this analysis, foreign trade leads to specialization; every country specializes in a subset of products and relies on other countries for the supply of goods and services it does not produce. Although this form of specialization is too extreme for applied analysis, it illustrates Ricardian comparative advantage in a sharp way. Moreover, here trade leads to specialization and *interdependence*. Mutual interdependence implies that events in one country affect its trade partners. Sometimes these effects are desirable, at other times not. To illustrate, consider a Dornbusch, Fischer, and Samuelson–type world, with England and Portugal being the two trading countries. Initially there is a relative wage at which every country specializes in a range of products according to its comparative advantage and all markets clear. Starting from this configuration, labor supply rises in England as a result, say, of more women joining the labor force. How does this affect wages and patterns of specialization? And is it beneficial or harmful to Portugal?

To understand the impact of growth in labor supply, first note that if relative wages were to remain at their initial level, patterns of specialization would not change because every country would remain the least-cost supplier of the same set of products as before. But under the circumstances, labor supply in England would exceed demand. It therefore follows that market balance now requires a higher wage in Portugal relative to England. But with a lower English relative wage it is cheaper to produce more products in England and fewer in Portugal. Naturally, whatever goods and services were more cheaply produced in England before are also more cheaply produced in England now. But there also exist products for which Portugal used to be the least-cost producer for which England now becomes the least-cost producer; their production moves from Portugal to England, thereby changing the patterns of specialization. This reallocation takes time, because Portuguese workers who had been employed in the displaced industries have to find employment in sectors in which Portugal still has a cost advantage, and new English workers have to find jobs in the newly acquired English industries as well as in other sectors in which England has a cost advantage. Eventually, however, more products are manufactured in England and fewer in Portugal.

Portugal's gain in relative wages improves the standard of living of Portuguese workers after the adjustment is complete (but not necessarily before that). The reason is that with the new wages they can buy the same quantities of goods that are still produced in Portugal, but they can afford to purchase more English products, including those whose production moved from Portugal to England. In other words, the purchasing power of Portuguese wages has increased. At the same time the purchasing power of English wages has declined. An English worker can buy with his new wages the same amounts of English products that were originally manufactured in England. Yet he can buy fewer products that were originally manufactured in Portugal, including those that are now manufactured in England. Naturally, new English workers, those who joined the labor force, gain income that they did not have before. But English workers who were previously employed lose from the expansion of the English labor force.

Another way to understand Portugal's gains from the expansion of the English labor force is to consider how the expansion impacts the relative prices of goods manufactured in the two countries. As a result of the rise in the wage rate of Portuguese workers relative to the wage rate of English workers, the prices of Portugal's exports rise relative to the prices of its imports, which economists call an improvement in the terms of trade.[19] Under the circumstances Portugal pays fewer exportables for every unit of its importables, enabling its residents to acquire more beneficial amounts of consumption. The understanding that exports are valuable because they pay for imports is an important ingredient in a broad assessment of international economic relations. Note that exports consist of goods and services that a country "gives away" to other countries. For this reason exports are not valuable per se, but rather via the quid pro quo of the exchange in which they pay for imports.[20]

I have described a development in one country—an expansion of its labor force—that improves its trade partner's well-being. Moreover, this event reduces the standard of living of the country's original workers. Naturally, not every development in one country impacts its trade partner in the same way, and not every development has an asymmetric effect on the prosperity of the trading partners. To illustrate the latter point, replace the expansion of labor in the previous example with an improvement in the productivity of English workers. In particular, suppose that this improvement affects all sectors equally, in the sense that if the amount of English labor required to manufacture leather products has declined by 5 percent so has the amount of English labor required to manufacture wood products. At one level this is similar to the expansion of England's labor supply, because the productivity improvement can be viewed as endowing England with *effectively* more labor. As a result, Portugal's workers gain, because the purchasing power of their wages rises. Unlike in the previous example, however, now England's wage rate per *effective* unit of labor declines, but not the wage per worker. Since every worker is endowed with more effective units of labor, what is relevant for well-being is not the worker's wage rate per effective unit but rather his compensation for all the effective units he has. This calculation shows that English workers gain from the productivity improvement; their wages rise in real terms. Evidently, in this case the development in England benefits all workers, English and Portuguese alike. It is a nice example of productivity-driven growth that benefits the growing country and its trade partner. The benefits to the trade partner are transmitted through an improvement in the partner's terms of trade.

Transport costs and other impediments to trade also play an important role in shaping world trade flows. For this reason it is important to account for them in any model that seeks to explain the data. Dornbusch, Fischer, and Samuelson (1977) suggested a simple formulation in which transport costs are proportional to production costs and the same factor of proportionality applies to all products.[21] Under these circumstances every country specializes in products in which it has the largest comparative advantage, while products in which neither country has a sufficiently large comparative advantage are not traded internationally; the nontraded products are manufactured in every country for local use only. Naturally, more products are not traded the higher the transport costs are.

A variety of studies have attempted to examine the extent to which Ricardo's insights are borne out by the data. The difficulty in this pursuit is to operationalize the empirical implications of Ricardo's theory for a world with many countries that trade with each other. Eaton and Kortum (2002) developed the most successful approach.[22] They consider a world with "melting iceberg" trade frictions that differ across pairs of trade partners (e.g., shipping goods from England to France can be more costly than shipping goods from Portugal to France). Moreover, they assume a specific distribution of labor productivity across products, which has two parameters: one that is country specific, the other shared by all countries.[23] The country-specific component is needed to account for total factor productivity (TFP) differences across countries, where TFP is a single measure of how efficient inputs are combined in production; it is very hard to fit to data a model that does not allow variation in TFP. The common component imposes a similar productivity dispersion across products in every country. While this is a major restriction, it reduces the number of parameters that have to be estimated. An important assumption is that productivity levels attained in one country are independent of productivity levels attained in another. Using these assumptions together with melting-iceberg trade costs, it is possible to calculate for every country the distribution of the minimum cost of sourcing products from all potential suppliers. These minimum costs determine domestic prices and the share of domestic spending on every country's output.[24] The resulting equations are then estimated on data from a sample of 19 Organisation for Economic Co-operation and Development (OECD) countries, and the estimates are used to quantitatively gauge various economic relationships.

To attain insight into one such relationship, consider Eaton and Kortum's simulation of a proportional improvement in U.S. technology. We discussed the implications of such an improvement in a two-country world, concluding that both countries—the technological winner and its trade partner—benefit. The mechanism through which the trade partner gains is an improvement in its terms of trade. The same channels of transmission operate in a multicountry world, except that with many trade partners the gains from improved terms of trade vary across countries, depending on a country's characteristics and its trade impediments with the technological winner. Figure 2.2 shows the results of the Eaton-Kortum simulation, depicted in the form of country welfare gains as

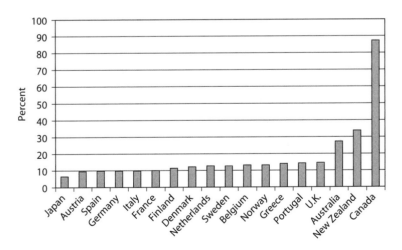

Figure 2.2. Fraction of welfare gains relative to the United States from a productivity improvement in the United States. Data from Eaton and Kortum (2002).

percentages of the U.S. welfare gain. Evidently, the welfare gains are not evenly distributed. Canada, which is a small country that has few impediments to trade with the U.S., gains more than any other country; its welfare gain is 87.4 percent of the U.S. welfare gain (where both are measured proportionately to the initial level of well-being). On the other side is Japan, whose welfare gain is only 6.6 percent of the U.S. gain. Australia and New Zealand also greatly benefit from U.S. technological improvements, while other countries gain less but derive substantial benefits nevertheless.

2.2 Factor Proportions

Ricardo's view of foreign trade dominated economic discourse for a whole century. Only in 1919 did a major challenge to his doctrine emerge. The charge was led by a Swedish economic historian by the name of Eli Heckscher, followed by his most distinguished student Bertil Ohlin.[25] Heckscher and Ohlin proposed replacing Ricardo's classical formulation of comparative advantage, based on the labor theory of value, with a neoclassical formulation, based on modern price theory, in which labor is treated on a par with other factors of production, such as capital and land. In this approach, factor proportions play center stage and differences across countries in the relative availability of factors of production are major determinants of patterns of specialization and trade.

Heckscher was interested in the impact of foreign trade on the distribution of income among factors of production. He therefore developed an economic model with labor, capital, and land as the primary inputs (or factors), and investigated how trade between two countries affects the rewards of these inputs. In the process he derived the implications of cross-country differences in factor endowments for the structure of trade. Although Heckscher did not use equations, his verbal analysis is precise.

Ohlin went one step further. In the words of Flam and Flanders (1991, p. 13), Ohlin's contribution "was to combine, creatively, the trade theory of Heckscher's famous paper with Walrasian formalization, which he learned from Cassel."[26] Indeed, in chapter 3 of his dissertation, titled "Mathematical Illustration," Ohlin spells out the equations that need to be satisfied in every trading country, allowing for many factors of production and many sectors. Moreover, he improves on Heckscher by allowing factor use per unit output to respond to factor prices, which Heckscher did not.

The basic logic of the Heckscher-Ohlin view of foreign trade can be seen by reexamining a world of two countries with many sectors, like the one discussed in the previous section. To bring in factor composition considerations, however, let there be two primary inputs, labor and capital, rather than only labor. Both Heckscher and Ohlin argue that technological possibilities are the same in all countries. By this they mean that everyone everywhere has access to the same choice of inputs per unit output. Absent economies or diseconomies of scale,[27] this implies that the unit cost of manufacturing depends on factor prices but not on the location of production. This is a major departure from Ricardo's view, in which the costs of goods vary across countries because relative labor requirements differ. In contrast, in the Heckscher-Ohlin view of the world, if two countries have the same factor prices they also have the same unit cost for each and every product, in which case no country has a relative cost advantage in any product. Two conditions have to be satisfied for trade to take place under these circumstances, and both are clearly stated by Heckscher:[28] "A difference in the relative scarcity of the factors of production between one country and the other is thus a necessary condition for differences in comparative costs and consequently for international trade. A further condition is that the proportions in which the factors of production are combined not be the same for one commodity as for another. In the absence of this second condition, the price of one commodity relative to that of another would be the same in all countries regardless of differences in relative factor prices" (Heckscher, 1919, in Flam and Flanders, 1991, p. 48). That is, factor prices should differ across countries and factor intensities should differ across sectors. If factor prices do not differ, the countries have the same costs in all industries. And if factor prices do differ but all products have the same composition of inputs (i.e., the same factor intensities) then the two countries have the same *relative* costs in all industries.

When discussing relative factor prices (relative scarcity), both Heckscher and Ohlin refer to the conditions prior to trade, when the countries are in isolation. They then point out that trade reduces the disparity in relative factor prices across countries, and that it may even eliminate all differences in factor prices (when measured in similar units), leading to factor price equalization.[29] For now, however, consider a situation in which our two countries, say England and Portugal, trade with each other without factor price equalization. As before, suppose that there are four industries: cloth, wood, leather, and wine. Moreover, suppose that cloth is the most capital-intensive product (i.e., it uses more capital per unit labor than the other three sectors); wood is the next most capital-intensive industry; and wine is the least capital-intensive. Also suppose that capital is cheaper in England and labor is cheaper in Portugal. Then the relative cost of manufacturing cloth—the most capital-intensive product—in England, as compared to Portugal, is lower than the relative cost of manufacturing any one of the other three goods in England. And the relative cost of manufacturing wood in England is lower than the relative cost of manufacturing leather or wine in England. And finally, the relative cost of manufacturing leather in England is lower than the relative cost of manufacturing wine.

These relative costs are depicted in Figure 2.3. Which country has a cost advantage in wood or leather depends now on the location of the break-even cost ratio 1 on the figure's vertical axis (i.e., the cost ratio at which the unit cost in England is the same as the unit cost in Portugal). If "1" happens to be between the bars of cloth and wood, then England specializes in cloth and Portugal specializes in wood, leather, and wine. If "1" happens to be between the bars of wood and leather, then England

Unit Cost in England

Unit Cost in Portugal

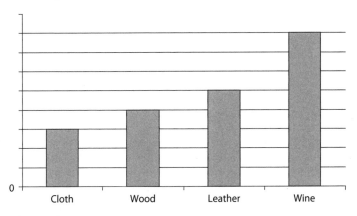

Figure 2.3. Relative unit costs in four industries.

specializes in cloth and wood while Portugal specializes in leather and wine. And if "1" happens to be between the bars of leather and wine, then Portugal specializes in wine and England specializes in the other three products. Naturally, "1" cannot be located below the bar of cloth or above the bar of wine, because in each of these cases one country has a cost advantage in all products and the other cannot profitably employ its labor and capital. Under the circumstances, factor prices will change, with the wage rate and the rental rate on capital declining in the country that has a cost disadvantage in all products. Therefore if the figure describes an equilibrium outcome, "1" has to be located somewhere between the bar of cloth and the bar of wine.

This analysis shows that the country with the relatively lower cost of capital specializes in capital-intensive products and the country with the relatively lower cost of labor specializes in labor-intensive products (or less-capital-intensive products). The precise cut in the chain of comparative costs determines the precise specialization pattern, but the qualitative features of the specialization pattern are independent of the location of this cut, in analogy with the Ricardian model of trade. Indeed, Dornbusch, Fischer, and Samuelson (1980) analyze a Heckscher-Ohlin model with many goods and fixed expenditure shares, showing how the cut in the chain of comparative costs is determined in general equilibrium. Importantly, the cut is determined simultaneously with the relative factor rewards in the two countries.

This begs the question of which country has the lowest cost of capital. In the absence of impediments to trade, international commerce equalizes commodity prices across countries. Therefore it has to be the case that the country with a larger endowment of capital relative to labor has a lower rental rate on capital and a higher wage rate, unless factor prices are equalized. Combining this observation with the previous arguments then implies that England, which has a higher ratio of capital to labor than Portugal, has the lower rental rate on capital and the higher wage rate. As a result, the prediction is that the country relatively abundant in capital exports capital-intensive products, while the country relatively abundant in labor exports labor-intensive products. This is known as the Heckscher-Ohlin Theorem. Ohlin's statement of this result cannot be clearer: "In short, commodities that embody large quantities of particularly scarce factors are imported, and commodities intensive in relatively abundant factors are exported" (Ohlin, 1924, p. 90 in Flam and Flanders, 1991).[30]

While my discussion centered on the pricing of goods and factors in the trading environment, both Heckscher and Ohlin focused their analysis on the pricing of goods and factors in autarky, when a country does not participate in foreign trade. In particular, they noted that the country that has the relatively lower autarky cost of capital will export capital-intensive products, and the country that has the relatively lower autarky cost of labor will export labor-intensive products. Although the two types of prediction—one based on pretrade factor prices, the other on posttrade factor prices—are not always the same, they coincide under a broad set of circumstances that have been clarified in the literature.[31]

I have discussed trade structure under the supposition that factor prices differ across countries and that these differences generate a ranking of relative costs. Yet both Heckscher and Ohlin pointed out the tendency of factor prices to converge in response to foreign trade. This tendency has been formally studied by later scholars, starting with the work of Samuelson (1948). Their main finding is that unimpeded international trade equalizes factor prices when differences in the factor composition of the trade partners are not too large. This is known as the Factor Price Equalization Theorem. Moreover, when all countries have the same homothetic preferences (i.e., their expenditure shares on various goods depend only on prices—which are the same when the countries trade with each other—but not on income), then every country exports products that are on average intensive in the factors of production with which the country is abundantly supplied and every country imports products that are on average intensive in the country's scarce factors of production.[32]

Factor price equalization played an important role in the development of the neoclassical theory of international trade. True, factor prices are not the same in every country, and there are very large differences in some factor prices, such as wages. Therefore it is evident that this model cannot adequately describe all aspects of reality. The more important question, however, is whether it depicts the structure of world trade reasonably well.[33]

To form a judgement, first consider Leamer's (1984) study, which examines a noteworthy implication of this model. He starts from the observation that whenever all countries can tap into the same pool of technologies and manufacturers everywhere face the same factor prices, then the employed composition of inputs per unit output in a given industry is the same in every country. Under the circumstances, every country's sectoral output levels are the same linear functions of their factor endowments, provided the output levels that secure full employment of the country's factors of production are uniquely determined.[34] That is to say, a country's output levels are determined by its factors of production, and the marginal effect of a factor of production on the output of a particular sector, say, leather products, is the same in every country. The latter means that if the addition of one unit of labor in England raises England's output of leather products by five units, then the addition of one unit of labor in Portugal raises Portugal's output of leather products by five units too. Leamer then combines this specification with the assumption that all countries have identical expenditure shares (i.e., if one country spends 10 percent of its income on food, so does every other country) to show that this implies that the net exports (the difference between exports and imports) of every sector are a linear function of the country's factor endowments.[35] This strong property of net export functions permits easy estimation of their coefficients. Some of the estimated marginal effects are presented in Table 2.1.[36]

The table shows that capital has a positive effect on net exports in all four manufacturing industries: labor-intensive manufactures, capital-intensive manufactures, machinery, and chemicals. At the same time, it has a negative impact on net exports in the remaining sectors: petroleum, raw materials, forest products, tropical products, and cereals.[37] Minerals impact net exports in the opposite direction in all sectors except for petroleum. This implies that countries with larger stocks of capital export,

Table 2.1.   Marginal Effects of Capital, Minerals, and Oil on Net Exports, 1975

	Capital	Minerals	Oil
Petroleum	−18.4	−0.4	0.6
Raw materials	−8.9	0.86	0.04
Forest products	−1.7	0.53	0.08
Tropical agriculture	−2.9	0.44	0.05
Animal products	−0.5	0.28	0.05
Cereals	−4.5	0.97	0.24
Labor-intensive manufactures	1.9	−0.09	−0.07
Capital-intensive manufactures	17.9	−0.46	−0.17
Machinery	29.1	−1.1	−0.27
Chemicals	4.1	−0.15	−0.04

Source: Leamer (1984, table 6.1).

on net, more manufactures and less petroleum, raw materials, and agriculture, while countries with larger mineral deposits export more raw materials and agriculture and less petroleum and manufactures. The table also shows that countries with larger oil deposits export less manufactures and more raw materials and agriculture, just as countries with more minerals do. Except that countries with more oil export, on net, more petroleum while countries with more minerals export less petroleum.[38]

As already explained, the linearity of the net export functions results from a combination of linear output functions and common expenditure shares. Neither of these assumptions describes reality accurately. Although consumption patterns are similar across many countries, substantial differences exist between poor and rich countries. For example, in 1975 Austria and Switzerland, two rich countries, spent about 20 percent of their income on food. In the same year India and the Philippines, which were much poorer, spent more than half their income on food (see Leamer, 1984, table 1.6). These numbers illustrate a well-known phenomenon: the budget share of food declines with income, that is, rich people spend on food proportionately less than poor people. When budget shares vary across countries as a result of differences in income per capita, consumption preferences become an independent source of trade flows. To see why, note that when a poor country trades with a rich one, the poor country has a disproportionately large demand for food, which biases its trade toward food imports independently of factor endowments. Similar arguments apply to other products whose budget shares depend on income. Hunter (1991) studied the impact of such preferences on trade and found that they can explain a substantial fraction of the trade volume.[39]

Although Leamer's derivation of linear net export functions requires the linearity of output functions, the Heckscher-Ohlin Theorem does not require this restriction. Nevertheless, linear output functions are prevalent.[40] The marginal effects of factor endowments on output levels are often referred to as Rybczynski coefficients, in honor of the British economist who first pointed out this relationship in a simple case of two industries and two factors of production (see Rybczynski, 1955). Suppose that the two factors of production are capital and labor. Then the Rybczynski Theorem states that an increase in the endowment of capital, holding constant the capital-labor ratio in each industry, will raise output disproportionately in the capital-intensive sector and contract output in the labor-intensive sector.[41] Similarly, an expansion of the labor force will raise output disproportionately in the labor-intensive sector and contract output in the capital-intensive sector. In other words, a country's output composition is biased toward the industry that is relatively intensive in the factor of production with which the country is relatively well endowed. When spending patterns are the same across the trade partners, this implies that trade is driven by biases in output composition and therefore by differences in relative factor endowments, as suggested by the Heckscher-Ohlin Theorem.[42]

Rybczynski's insight was extended by Jones and Scheinkman (1977) to the case of many sectors and many factors of production. The main result is that the growth of a factor endowment, holding constant the techniques of production in every sector (i.e., the composition of factors of production per unit output), leads to a disproportionate expansion of some industries and to a contraction of others. Unlike the simple two-sector two-factor case, there exists no good ranking of sectors by factor intensity in the general case, and therefore no clear affiliation of sectors with factors of production that will enable us to state that one sector is the most capital-intensive, another the most unskilled-labor–intensive, and a third the most arable-land–intensive. Yet every factor is a compatriot of some sector, whose output expands when the factor grows, and every factor is an adversary of some other sector, which is forced to contract when that factor grows. The empirical implication is that estimates of Rybczynski coefficients should have the following property: every factor of production should have positive effects on some output levels and negative effects on others, similar to the effects of factors of production on trade flows in

Table 2.1. This pattern has indeed been found in empirical studies. For example, Fitzgerald and Hallak (2004) estimate Rybczynski coefficients for capital, skilled labor, unskilled labor, and arable land. They find that capital is a compatriot of wood products and an adversary of textiles, while arable land is a compatriot of nonferrous metals and an adversary of electric machinery (see their table 4).[43]

Although the research described here has unveiled interesting patterns of international specialization and trade, it has not directly tested the Heckscher-Ohlin Theorem. According to this theorem, a country should export products that are intensive in the country's relatively abundant factors of production and import products that are intensive in the country's relatively scarce factors of production. Evidently, to test this prediction it is necessary to study the impact of factor endowments on trade flows, accounting for the factor intensity of the importing and exporting sectors, but this last element is missing from the studies just mentioned.

Direct tests of the three-way relationship between factor endowments, factor intensity, and trade patterns were hard to come by. As a result, an alternative approach—that uses the key three-way relationship indirectly—was formulated: the factor content approach. Instead of examining directly exports and imports of products, this approach—which has its origin in Ohlin's dissertation—examines the implied exports and imports of factor services embodied in the traded products. Ohlin stated that "each region comes to be engaged in the production of those goods that it can produce at lower cost than others, that is, those goods intensive in its low-priced factors of production. Again, those commodities requiring large amounts of the relatively scarce factors will be imported from regions where those factors are less scarce. Indirectly therefore abundant factors of production are exported and scarce factors imported" (Ohlin, 1924, p. 91 in Flam and Flanders, 1991). The key lies in the last sentence, where Ohlin states that international trade in products serves as an indirect means of trading factors of production, or more accurately, the services of factors of production. When factors of production are not mobile across countries while goods are mobile, trade in goods enables countries to exchange indirectly services of factors of production, every country importing the services of its scarce factors and exporting the services of its abundant factors.

Wassily Leontief, the developer of input-output tables, was the first to note the empirical potential of what became known as the "factor content" view of international trade flows. In a paper read in 1953 to the American Philosophical Society, he examined the labor content and capital content of America's 1947 trade flows (see Leontief, 1953). Using his input-output tables, Leontief calculated that $1 million worth of U.S. exports embodied directly and indirectly the services of $2,550,780 worth of capital and 182.3 man-years of labor. In other words, the capital-labor ratio in U.S. exports was close to $14,000 of capital per man-year. In the same year, based on the U.S. input-output tables, $1 million of U.S. imports embodied directly and indirectly the services of $3,091,339 worth of capital and 170 man-years of labor. As a result, the capital-labor ratio embodied in U.S. imports was a little over $18,000 of capital per man-year, significantly larger than the capital-labor ratio in U.S. exports. These results can be viewed as contradicting the prediction of the factor proportions trade theory, because the United States had by far the highest ratio of capital to labor in the immediate post–World War II period and should therefore have exported capital-intensive products and imported labor-intensive products, while Leontief's calculations showed the opposite. This has become known as the Leontief Paradox.

Before discussing the Leontief Paradox, it is necessary to better understand the factor content view of international trade flows, which is formulated in the sharpest form in Vanek (1968). Vanek imagines a world of many countries and many factors of production. All countries have access to the same constant-returns-to-scale technologies (i.e., technologies in which a proportional increase in all inputs raises output by the same factor of proportionality) and all choose the same composition of consumption when faced with the same relative prices (i.e., all have the same homothetic preferences). The countries trade with each other without impediment, and factor prices consequently are equalized.[44] As a result, input use per unit output is the same in every country. This means that the composition of inputs used by the United States to produce one unit of cloth is the same as the composition of inputs used to produce one unit of cloth in England, Portugal, France, or any other country. These input requirements differ across sectors, yet in a given industry they do not differ across countries. Under these circumstances every country has the same input-output table.

Naturally, the assumptions of identical input-output tables and equalization of factor prices conflict with the data. Not only do wages and capital rental rates differ across countries, so do the input-output tables of the OECD countries, which are at a similar level of development (see Trefler, 1993 and Hakura, 2001). Input-output tables differ even more between the developed and the developing countries. Nevertheless, Vanek's system is useful because it has clear implications that can be tested with available data sets. In particular, it uniquely predicts the factor content of trade flows.[45] Here is why.

Since every country uses the same inputs to produce a given product, we can use the common coefficients of the input-output table to compute the factor content of a country's imports and exports. Consider, for example, wheat and cloth, which use land and capital in production. We can calculate the total amount of land services embodied in U.S. exports of these products by multiplying land use per unit of wheat with the export of wheat, and add to it land use per unit cloth times the export of cloth. And we can similarly calculate the total amount of capital embodied in these exports by multiplying capital use per unit wheat with the export of wheat, and add to it capital use per unit cloth times the export of cloth. More generally, we can calculate the total use of land in U.S. exports as the sum across all sectors of land use per unit output times the export level, and we can calculate the total use of capital as the sum across all sectors of capital use per unit output times the export level. Similar calculations can be done for every factor of production to arrive at an estimate of the total amount of its use in the economy's exports. Following a similar procedure we can also calculate the factor content of U.S. imports. The difference between the factor content of exports and the factor content of imports yields an estimate of the factor content of U.S. *net* exports. When a particular input has a positive difference, say human capital, it implies that the United States exports the services of this input on net. And when the difference is negative, it implies that the United States imports the services of this input on net. These calculations represent the net flows of factor services *embodied* in the imports and exports of all products.

Information about trade flows and technology is contained in calculations of the factor content of net exports, including sectoral factor intensities. Vanek's great achievement was showing that under the model's assumptions the factor content of net exports has to equal the difference between the country's factor endowments and its pro rata share of the world's factor endowments. For the United States, for example, this implies that if U.S. spending equals 25 percent of total world spending, then the arable-land content of its net exports has to equal the U.S. endowment of arable land minus a quarter of the world's endowment of arable land; the unskilled-labor content of its net exports has to equal the U.S. endowment of unskilled labor minus a quarter of the world's endowment of unskilled labor; and so on. And this remarkable set of relationships has to be satisfied by every factor endowment in every country.

The logic behind Vanek's equations is the following. Net exports of a product equal domestic production minus domestic consumption.[46] Therefore the factor content of net exports has to equal the factor content of domestic production minus the factor content of domestic consumption. In an economy with full employment, the factor content of domestic production equals the economy's factor endowment. Therefore the factor content of net exports equals the domestic factor endowment minus the factor content of domestic consumption. Now, with homothetic preferences all countries have the same composition of consumption. Therefore, given identical factor use per unit output in all countries, the *composition* of inputs embodied in a country's consumption is the same everywhere and the only differences arise from the scale of consumption; some countries spend more than others and therefore have proportionately more inputs embodied in their consumption. Under these circumstances, the total amount of factors of production embodied in the world's consumption equals the world's endowment of factors of production. As a result, every country's factor content of consumption is a fraction of the world's endowment of factors of production, and this fraction equals the country's share in total world spending. Hence the Vanek equations.

Vanek's equations link all three elements of the factor proportions theory: factor endowments, factor intensities, and trade flows. For this reason they provide a convenient framework for testing the theory. Leamer (1980) used these equations to reexamine Leontief's data. He pointed out that with balanced trade, or nearly balanced trade, the factor content of net exports of some inputs has to be positive and the factor content of others has to be negative. In other words, the services of some factors of production have to be exported on net while the services of others have to be imported. In a world with only two inputs, say labor and capital, this implies that if labor services are exported on net then capital services are imported, and if labor services are imported on net then capital services are exported. In the former case, the capital-labor ratio embodied in exports is smaller than the capital-labor ratio embodied in imports, while in the latter case the opposite is true. As a result, Leontief's calculations contradict the supposition that the United States was capital-rich in 1947 if labor and capital were the only two factors of production. Naturally, labor and capital were not the only two factors of production. In addition to different types of land and natural resources, there are different types of labor, such as skilled and unskilled, and different types of capital, such as machines and structures. It is therefore not necessary for one of these two inputs, capital or labor, to be exported on net and for the other to be imported. In fact, in Leontief's data the

United States exported over $23 billion worth of capital on net and close to 2 billion man-years on net. That is, the United States exported both capital and labor services. With net exports of both capital and labor, the United States could be capital-rich even when its capital-labor ratio in imports exceeds its capital-labor ratio in exports if the ratio of its *net* capital exports relative to its *net* labor exports exceeds the ratio of capital to labor embodied in its consumption. Leamer calculated that the ratio of net capital exports to net labor exports was close to $12,000 per man-year, while the capital-labor ratio in consumption was close to $7,000 per man-year, in which case this condition is met. Therefore there is nothing paradoxical in Leontief's finding; the United States could be capital-rich in 1947 and nevertheless have a higher ratio of capital to labor in its imports than in its exports.[47]

Leamer's analysis pointed out how theory can be used to interpret evidence, but it did not provide a test of the factor proportions theory. Under the maintained hypothesis that the theory is correct, he derived conditions that squared Leontief's evidence with the notion that the United States was capital-rich in 1947. To test the theory, however, it is necessary to match the variation in Vanek's measures of factor abundance (i.e., the difference between a country's factor endowments and its pro rata share of the world's factor endowments) with the variation in the factor content of net exports. For this, one needs data on trade flows and endowments for a large enough sample of countries. A first test of this type is provided in Bowen, Leamer, and Sveikauskas (1987). They use 12 factors and 27 countries to compute the factor content of net exports and the factor abundance measures in 1967, using the U.S. input-output table as a common technology matrix. And they find a poor fit between the factor content of net exports and the measures of factor abundance. Rough tests that examine the degree to which the signs of the factor content and factor abundance measures match (i.e., whether a factor content is positive [negative] when the factor abundance measure is positive [negative]), or whether they are similarly ranked, do not perform well; the sign test is violated in about one-third of the cases and the rank-order test is violated in about half the cases. In other words, the Vanek equations do not provide a good description of these data.

Trefler (1995) repeated the Bowen, Leamer, and Sveikauskas analysis on a data set consisting of 33 countries and 9 inputs in 1983, and reached a similar conclusion. He identified, however, the sources of the mismatch between the factor content and factor abundance measures. First, the factor content measures are systematically too small in absolute values in comparison to the factor abundance measures. This means that trade predicted by differences in factor endowments greatly exceeds observed trade in factor services, a phenomenon known as "missing trade." Second, for poor countries the factor abundance measures overpredict the factor content of net exports more than for rich countries. It therefore appears that poor countries do not export enough factor content and they import too much factor content in comparison to rich countries. Finally, poor countries appear to be abundant in more inputs than rich countries. These findings suggest that productivity levels may differ across countries, contrary to the assumption of the theoretical model. If developing countries are less productive than developed countries, then standard measures of factor endowments overstate the effective quantities of their inputs in comparison to the rich countries; this overstatement can explain the second and third features of the data. In other words, the assumption that all countries can tap into the same technology pool is too strong. Indeed, plenty of evidence suggests that total factor productivity (TFP) differs greatly across countries (see Dollar and Wolff, 1993, and Helpman, 2004), and even among the seven richest economies—which are close to each other in levels of development—there are substantial differences in TFP (see Helpman, 2004).

To examine the explanatory power of productivity differences, Trefler (1995) develops two modified versions of the Vanek equations. In one version he allows Hicks-neutral TFP differences across countries; that is, he allows countries to differ in a proportional manner in the efficiency with which they deploy inputs. This means that if, say, the U.S. is 20 percent more efficient than Italy in the use of a particular combination of inputs, in the sense that the U.S. produces 20 percent more output with these inputs, then the U.S. is also 20 percent more efficient than Italy in the use of all other possible combinations of these inputs. In the second version he divides the countries into two groups: North, consisting of a group of countries with high income per capita, and South, consisting of poorer countries. The rich countries are assumed to share the same technology as the United States. The poorer countries also share a common technology, except that theirs differs from the U.S. technology in a factor-biased fashion; in South every factor of production can be less productive than in North to a different degree. This means that if it takes two hours for a high-school graduate from a Southern country to contribute to production as much as it takes one hour for a high-school graduate from the United States, then this two-to-one ratio also applies to high-school graduates from all other Southern countries. Moreover, it also means that the ratio can differ for college graduates. For example, it may be the case that it takes three hours for a college graduate from a Southern country to contribute to production as much as it takes one hour for a U.S. college graduate to contribute. Now factor price equalization can still hold, but only if applied to the *effective* units of every input. In the example of the high-school graduates, factor price equalization of effective units implies that a high-school graduate earns in South half the wage that a high-school graduate earns in North.[48]

Estimating both versions of the model, Trefler finds that the Hicks-neutral version of technology differences performs better. With this modification in place, the mismatch between the factor content and factor abundance measures is much smaller but substantial nevertheless. In other words, differences in technology help explain the data, but not enough to eliminate the "missing trade."

It became clear in the course of this research that the assumptions embodied in the theoretical models are too strong for data analysis. Trefler

(1995) has shown that at a minimum one has to allow proportional differences in TFP across countries, while Hakura (2001) has shown that using individual country input-output tables to calculate the factor content of exports (not net exports) greatly improves the fit with the data.

Differences across countries in factor use per unit output can arise from two sources: variation in technology and variation in factor prices. Both are potentially important. Indeed, differences in factor prices can bias the factor content of net exports toward zero, as Trefler has found in the data. To see why, consider labor and capital, and suppose that capital is cheaper and labor is more expensive in the United States than in other countries. Then the calculation of the factor content of U.S. exports, using the U.S. input-output table, provides the correct measures for the United States. But calculating the factor content of U.S. imports using the U.S. input-output table provides a biased measure, because as a result of factor price differences, the other countries use less capital and more labor per unit output than the United States. As a result, estimates of the factor content of U.S. net exports that are obtained from the U.S. input-output table underestimate the capital content and overestimate the labor content of net exports. In this event it will appear that the United States exports too little capital and imports too little labor as compared to its factor abundance measures. Davis and Weinstein (2001) find that correcting the factor content measures for the impact of differences across countries in the availability of labor and capital significantly improves their match with the factor abundance measures. Moreover, accounting for intermediate inputs and the presence of nontraded goods also improves the fit. In sum, allowing for Hicks-neutral technology differences, for the impact of factor endowments on factor prices and thereby on the input-output coefficients, for intermediate inputs, and for nontraded goods jointly explains the data reasonably well.[49]

3

Gainers and Losers

Smith and Ricardo believed that specialization and trade benefit all parties to an exchange. Ricardo in particular extended this view to countries, arguing that trade restrictions are harmful. He was engaged in a debate concerning the Corn Laws, a major piece of protectionist legislation that was passed in the British parliament by the landed aristocracy in 1815, two years before the publication of his magnum opus *The Principles of Political Economy and Taxation*.[50] In fact, Ricardo developed his theory of comparative advantage to illustrate the benefits of free trade.

Recall Ricardo's example of trade in cloth and wine: it takes England the labor of 100 man-years to produce a certain amount of cloth that takes Portugal the labor of only 90 man-years to produce; and it takes England 120 man-years to produce a certain amount of wine that takes Portugal only 80 man-years to produce. For concreteness, let us choose units of measurement so that the amount of cloth produced in this example is 100 and the amount of wine is 120. Since labor use per unit output is constant in the production of both goods, this implies that an English worker can produce in one year one unit of cloth or one unit of wine, while a Portuguese worker can produce in one year $\frac{10}{9}$ units of cloth or 1.5 units of wine. Therefore, England can convert one unit of cloth into one unit of wine by moving a worker for one year from cloth production to wine production, while Portugal can convert one unit of cloth into 1.35 units of wine by moving a worker from cloth to wine production for $\frac{9}{10}$ of a year. Under these circumstances the price of cloth is the same as the price of wine in England and the price of cloth exceeds by 35 percent the price of wine in Portugal, when the two countries do not trade. And the price of cloth is at least as high as the price of wine but by no more than 35 percent, when the two countries trade with each other.

For illustrative purposes, suppose that the price of cloth exceeds the price of wine by 20 percent when the two countries trade. The reasoning behind the gains from trade can now be described as follows. When England does not trade, it produces certain amounts of cloth and wine, the wine being equally expensive as cloth. By opening to trade, England can specialize in the production of cloth and buy all its wine from Portugal. In particular, suppose England keeps all the cloth it used to consume in autarky and sells to Portugal the remaining output. Since in the exchange with Portugal cloth costs 20 percent more than wine, England obtains from Portugal 1.2 times more wine than its workers produced in autarky. In this event the English enjoy the same amount of cloth they used to have in autarky and they drink more wine. Moreover, by selling to Portugal a little less cloth than suggested above, the English can have both more wine and more cloth. In other words, trading with Portugal makes available consumption possibilities that surpass autarky consumption levels. The expansion of consumption possibilities in the vicinity of the autarky consumption basket is the key to gains from trade, and it generalizes to economies with much more complex production structures. A similar argument applies to Portugal, which by specializing in wine can realize consumption possibilities that yield more cloth and more wine than its autarky consumption levels. More generally, trade yields better consumption possibilities when countries specialize according to comparative advantage.

To complete the argument, it is necessary to show that better consumption possibilities make trade gainful. In other words, a country cannot have lower welfare when it avails itself of consumption opportunities that yield higher welfare levels. Although this part of the argument can be perceived by some as trivial, because they cannot imagine that good opportunities would be missed, it is in fact far from obvious. First, the argument requires a clear statement of what we mean by a *country's* welfare. Second, some deep economic insights are needed to prove it, even in the simplest of cases. The reason is that the allocation of productive resources, income levels, and consumption opportunities are all governed by market forces. For this reason the question is not just whether preferred outcomes become available, but also whether they can be delivered by market forces (see Chapter 4).

In the rest of this chapter I discuss these issues in greater detail, emphasizing distributional conflicts between gainers and losers. Before analyzing these conflicts, however, I explain the general results on gains from trade for economies with no distributional considerations.

3.1 No Distributional Conflicts

Consider a country that operates in autarky. As a result, domestic consumption equals domestic production of every good. Output levels result from the allocation of productive resources to various activities and their employment with the country's technological know-how. At this point we place no restrictions on the nature of the goods, preferences, inputs, or technology.

Next suppose that an opportunity arises to trade with other countries. The first question is whether this opportunity expands consumption possibilities in the vicinity of the autarky consumption levels. For this purpose imagine that a central authority that has all the information about productive opportunities and individual preferences takes control of the country's economy. Then this authority can choose not to trade with other countries and to allocate to every individual the consumption basket and employment duties the individual had in autarky. Obviously, under these circumstances every individual is as well off in the new state as she was in autarky.[51] In other words, the trading opportunities include the autarky outcome.

Starting from this point of departure, the central authority can explore two options. First, it can freeze the autarky employment and output levels while examining the exchange opportunities of goods with other countries. It may then find beneficial trades, in the sense that by selling to foreigners certain products in exchange for other products it can make all individuals in the economy better off. As an illustration, suppose that—among many other products—all individuals in this economy consume pasta and cheese, and that it is possible to exchange one pound of pasta for one pound of cheese with foreign countries. Then, by reducing the consumption of pasta by one pound and raising the consumption of cheese by one pound, the central authority may find a way to make all individuals better off. And if this does not work, then the opposite trade can be examined, that is, reducing the consumption of cheese by one pound and raising the consumption of pasta by one pound. It is quite likely that one of these trades will prove beneficial. Naturally, more complex exchanges can also be contemplated in the hope of finding one that makes all individuals better off.

Second, the central authority can cut the production of some products and raise the production of others by shifting resources from the former activities to the latter. To illustrate, think again about pasta and cheese. The central authority can take some of the factors of production employed in the production of pasta and assign them to manufacture cheese. For concreteness, suppose that by reducing the output of pasta by two pounds the central authority can raise the output of cheese by one pound. Naturally, if cheese can be exchanged for pasta with foreigners pound for pound, this sort of resource reallocation is not a good deal. However, in this case the reverse reallocation is a good deal. Namely, to move resources from the production of cheese to the production of pasta. By moving resources from cheese to pasta production, the central authority can give up a pound of cheese and gain two pounds of pasta.[52] Then it can sell the two pounds of pasta to foreigners in exchange for two pounds of cheese. As a result, it will have the same amounts of all goods as there were in autarky, except for cheese, of which there will be an extra pound. This extra pound of cheese can then be distributed to every individual to benefit them all. Moreover, it is clear from this argument that not only can the central authority secure more cheese consumption, it also can secure more consumption of all other goods by exchanging some of the extra pound of cheese for other products. Under the circumstances, the larger quantities of goods can be distributed to individuals so as to make everyone better off than in autarky.

This illustrates how more goods can be made available for consumption when the country engages in international trade and how they can be used to raise everyone's welfare.[53] The big question is this: Does the availability of welfare-improving outcomes ensure the realization of such an aftermath in a market economy, in which the allocation of resources is governed by the market mechanism? And can it be achieved with or without market-mediated government policies, such as taxes and subsidies? Because after all, we are interested in market economies, which represent the prevalent organizational mode of economic activity. The answer is yes, under some circumstances.

A neoclassical economy with identical individuals provides a useful benchmark. In this type of economy, technologies exhibit declining marginal productivity of inputs (i.e., the more of an input becomes available, the less the last unit of the input contributes to output), property rights are well defined, there are no externalities (i.e., no firm or individual directly benefits or is harmed by the activities of another firm or individual), and there is competition in product and factor markets (i.e., all firms and individuals are price takers in the sense that they view prices as determined independently of their own activities). Such an economy has a competitive equilibrium, and by the first theorem of welfare economics this equilibrium is Pareto efficient. The latter means that there is no feasible way to change the allocation of resources so as to make everyone better off (see Arrow and Hahn, 1971). In this type of economy all individuals are equally well off, because they all have the same preferences and they own identical combinations of productive resources.[54]

Now imagine that every country has these features. In particular, every country is populated by individuals with identical labor supply, preferences, and ownership of assets, although the individuals can differ across countries. Then the first theorem of welfare economics implies that every individual is at least as well off in the trade equilibrium as in autarky.[55] Here is why: when a country chooses to engage in international trade, it avails itself of the option to exchange products at the going international prices. In the example of pasta and cheese these prices allow it to exchange a pound of pasta for a pound of cheese. More generally, trade allows a country to transform one set of goods into another set, analogously to a production process. Thus, with the above prices of pasta and cheese the country can transform a pound of pasta into a pound of cheese, or vice versa. This is similar to a production process in which pasta is an input and cheese is an output, or cheese is an input and pasta is an output. For this reason one can think about international trade as the expansion of production possibilities, where international prices determine the rates at which various goods can be transformed into other goods.[56] Viewed in this way, international trade cannot reduce welfare. The reason is that when a country trades, its competitive equilibrium is Pareto efficient under the supposition that the conversion rates of goods via trade are constant, because—given these conversion rates (prices)—it is always feasible not to trade and to attain the autarky welfare level.[57] Therefore welfare in the trade equilibrium is at least as high as in autarky. Moreover, the argument that by utilizing foreign trade a central authority can make more of every good available implies that individuals are, in fact, strictly better off in the trade equilibrium, which is Pareto efficient for the given international prices.

The conclusion that everyone gains from trade with no government intervention rests crucially on the assumption that all individuals are alike. As we shall see, when individuals differ from each other, trade may be harmful to some. Yet even in this case there are ways in which the government can intervene to secure gains from trade for all.

3.2 Two Case Studies

It is nearly impossible to obtain data on autarky regimes. This makes it difficult to estimate gains from trade. For this reason economists focus instead on the welfare effects of various trade policies that differ in their degree of restrictiveness but that do not come close to complete elimination of trade flows. Estimates of welfare losses from these restrictions cannot be used, however, to reliably project the results of complete exclusion from international markets. Nevertheless, there exist two historical episodes that provide good approximations to moves from trade to autarky and from autarky to trade: the U.S. trade embargo of 1807–1809 and Japan's opening up in 1859, respectively. In both cases the data are good enough to gauge the welfare costs of autarky, or the gains from trade.

3.2.1 The United States

Following a period of British harassment of U.S. vessels at sea during the Napoleonic wars—which was part of Britain's effort to blockade the continent and prevent shipments from neutral countries to France— President Jefferson convinced Congress to impose an embargo on U.S. trade. According to Irwin (2005, p. 632), "The British navy patrolled the eastern US coast and regularly intercepted American vessels, conducted searches and seizures, confiscated ships, cargos, and other property, and even impressed sailors (said to be British subjects) who were evading military service." The aim of the embargo was to punish Britain and to induce it to change its naval policy. The embargo, which started in December 1807, did not achieve this aim and was repealed after fourteen months, in March 1809.

The historical evidence is that the embargo was very effective in preventing trade flows, although it did not reduce them to zero. For example, the tonnage of American shipments to British ports declined by 80 percent, U.S. domestic merchandise exports declined from $48.7 million in 1807 to $9.4 million in 1808, and U.S. imports for domestic consumption declined from $85.1 million in 1807 to $45.1 million in 1808 (see Irwin, 2005).

U.S. commodity exports were concentrated in raw cotton, flour, tobacco, and rice, while its imports were much more diversified. The export-weighted average of the domestic prices of these four major exportables declined by 27 percent in less than a year, while the price index of importables increased toward the end of the embargo period by more than 30 percent. Evidently, the embargo worsened substantially the U.S. terms of trade.

Irwin (2005) calculates a theory-based measure of the welfare losses from this trade restriction, and finds that its major component—the value of net imports evaluated at the post-embargo prices—amounts to $46.9 million. When accounting for additional welfare components, this figure is adjusted downward to $33.1 million, amounting to 4.9 percent of gross national product (GNP). This is Irwin's central estimate.[58] Since the embargo was not complete, 4.9 percent of GNP is a lower bound on the gains from trade. It suggests that Jefferson's policy was very costly to the U.S. economy. Given this high cost and the lack of effectiveness of the embargo in changing Britain's policy, it is not surprising that the embargo was repealed after a short time.

3.2.2 Japan

The Tokugawa rulers of Japan adopted a policy of near autarky in 1639, and this policy prevailed for more than 200 years, until 1859. Following a period of upheaval until the Meiji Restoration in 1868, Japan expanded its commerce with foreign countries even more rapidly. According to some estimates, its imports per capita expanded a hundred fold through the early 1870s (see Bernhofen and Brown, 2005). During the 1870s, most of Japan's exports by value consisted of silk and tea, while its imports were more diverse and included iron, rails and rolling stock, machinery, woolen products, cotton products, raw sugar, and more. Some of these importables were not manufactured in Japan.

Between 1846–1855 and 1871–1879 the prices of Japan's major exportables increased substantially relative to the world. In particular, the price of its raw silk increased by 26 percent, the price of its cheap tea increased by 50 percent, and the price of its expensive tea increased by 64 percent, thereby substantially closing the gap in prices between Japan and the rest of the world (see Huber, 1971). Moreover, Japan's prices of importables converged toward world prices, and Huber calculates that Japan's terms of trade (i.e., the price index of exportables relative to import-competing products) increased 3.5-fold, a very large improvement indeed. At the same time, Japan's integration into the international commercial system had a minor effect on world prices. Using these data together with data on urban wages in Edo (today's Tokyo), Huber estimates gains from trade of the order of 65 percent of real national income.

Huber's estimate has been criticized, both for its methodology and for the use of Edo's wage data.[59] In contrast, a more satisfying analysis, which derives a theory-based upper bound on Japan's gains from trade, is provided in Bernhofen and Brown (2005). They show that the welfare gains from opening up to trade cannot exceed the value of the sectoral net imports (i.e., imports minus exports), evaluated at autarky prices. This upper bound is tight if trade does not impact sectoral output levels much, or if—more generally—GDP in autarky does not exceed by much the value of output in the trade equilibrium, when the trade equilibrium sectoral output levels are evaluated with autarky prices.[60] Lack of GDP data makes it difficult to assess the value of these estimated gains relative to Japan's income level. However, for a range of reasonable income levels, Bernhofen and Brown find that the upper bound on the gains from trade varies between 5.4 percent and 9.1 percent of GDP. True, these are much lower than Huber's estimate, but they are large nevertheless.

The Japanese case is interesting because the data on autarky prices are reliable, and the opening to trade was rapid. Under the circumstances the changes in prices and trade volumes in the 1860s can reasonably be attributed to trade as opposed to other causes, such as changes in technology or factor endowments.

The gains from trade discussed in this chapter emanate from the ability of open economies to export at higher prices and import at lower prices than in autarky. As intuitive as these sources of gains from trade are, the proof of their potency requires sophisticated analysis, because it is not obvious how market forces—when left to their own devices—accomplish the desired outcomes. Yet, once it is understood that trade allows countries to buy cheap and sell dear, this insight has an immediate implication for the structure of trade flows: we expect countries to import products that are expensive to produce in autarky in comparison to their trade prices, and to export products that are cheap to produce in autarky in comparison to their trade prices. In economies with many sectors and complicated technologies, this prediction does not apply to every single product, because unit costs of different goods are interrelated in complex ways. Nonetheless, Deardorff (1980) and Dixit and Norman (1980) show that this relationship has to hold on average. In particular, when a country moves from autarky to trade, the resulting changes in commodity prices have to be negatively correlated with net imports, or, what amounts to the same thing, the resulting changes in commodity prices have to be positively correlated with net exports. This means that, on average, the country imports products whose prices fall and exports products whose prices rise.

Bernhofen and Brown (2004) test this prediction with Japanese data from the mid-nineteenth century, when it opened to foreign commerce.

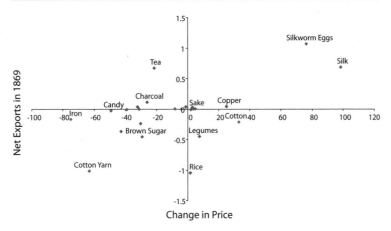

Figure 3.1. Price Changes and Net Exports in Japan, 1869. Data from Bernhofen and Brown (2004).

Figure 3.1 reproduces their main finding; it shows a clear positive correlation between price increases and net exports, as suggested by the Deardorff-Dixit-Norman result.[61] On average, Japan exported products whose prices increased when trade opened up and imported products whose prices declined.

3.3 Distributional Conflicts

Typically, when a country's residents are not all alike, distributional conflicts exist that color individual attitudes toward trade. These attitudes vary across individuals by economic status and employment characteristics, and they are related to the impact of trade on their incomes (see O'Rourke and Sinnott, 2001; Scheve and Slaughter, 2001; and Mayda and Rodrik, 2005). To understand the variation in these attitudes, it is necessary to understand how trade affects the distribution of income.

In Ricardo's world no distributional conflicts exist because his assumptions ensure that all income accrues to workers and all workers are equally paid. As a result, all workers gain from trade, even if they have different consumption preferences.[62] Evidently, in order to introduce a distributional conflict it is necessary to distinguish between different types of workers, or between labor and other factors of production, such as capital and land.

To illustrate, consider an alternative to Ricardo's example of trade in cloth and wine between England and Portugal, in which every country has two types of workers: cloth specialists and wine specialists. Cloth specialists do not know how to produce wine and wine specialists do not know how to produce cloth. This is obviously an extreme assumption concerning the imperfect substitutability of workers, which is just the opposite from the other extreme assumption of perfect substitutability adopted by Ricardo. Similar to Ricardo's world, however, assume that output per worker is constant within every industry, although it may differ across industries and countries.

In this world the output levels of every country are determined by the supply of specialized workers and by their productivity. The wage rate of cloth specialists is determined by the value of cloth output per cloth worker, and the wage rate of wine specialists is determine by the value of wine output per wine worker. Importantly, these output levels are the same in autarky and in the trading regime.

For concreteness, let the price of wine be higher than the price of cloth by 50 percent in England and by 35 percent in Portugal when the two countries do not trade. The exact numbers we use here are not important; the only important thing is that wine is relatively more expensive in England. The 50 percent premium on the price of wine has to ensure that the demand for cloth by Englishmen just equals the supply of cloth and the demand for wine equals the supply of wine, and the 35 percent premium on the price of wine in Portugal has to ensure market clearing in Portugal.

Next consider trade between the two countries. When they trade, the price of wine has to be between 35 percent to 50 percent higher than the price of cloth.[63] Assume that it is 40 percent higher. Under these circumstances England imports wine and exports cloth while Portugal exports wine and imports cloth. And in this equilibrium English cloth specialists are better off than in autarky while English wine specialists are worse off, and Portuguese cloth specialists are worse off than in autarky while Portuguese wine specialists are better off. In other words, in every country the factor of production that specializes in the import-competing industry loses from trade while the factor of production that specializes in the exporting industry gains. In this example there is a distributional conflict in every country between its import-allied and export-allied specialists. The example makes this conflict stark indeed.

To understand how the conflict arises, consider England; its cloth specialists earn a wage whose purchasing power is fixed in terms of cloth while its wine specialists earn a wage whose purchasing power is fixed in terms of wine. The cloth-wage of the cloth specialists (i.e., the amount of cloth they can purchase with their wages) is the same in autarky as in the trading equilibrium, and the wine-wage of the wine specialists (i.e., the amount of wine they can purchase with their wages) is the same in autarky as in the trading equilibrium. However, the wine-wage of the cloth specialists differs between trade and autarky, and the cloth-wage of the wine specialists also differs across these regimes. Since in autarky wine is 50 percent more expensive than cloth while in trade it is only 40 percent more expensive, the cloth specialists can purchase in the trading regime more of both goods than in autarky. By the same token the purchasing power of the wages of wine specialists is lower in the trading regime, because in this regime their wages can buy the same amount of wine as in autarky but less cloth. It follows that the cloth specialists gain from trade while the wine specialists lose. An analogous argument for Portugal shows that its wine specialists gain from trade while its cloth specialists lose. In summary, in every country the export-allied specialists gain from trade while the import-allied specialists lose.

While extreme, this example illustrates a broader point: factors of production that are allied with import-competing industries tend to lose from trade while factors of production that are allied with exporting industries tend to gain. In the example the alliance is extreme; one input is trapped in the import-competing sector, another input is trapped in the exporting sector. The mechanism through which these gains and losses materialize is a change in relative prices, which feeds into real incomes of inputs. An opening to international trade raises the relative price of exportables and reduces the relative price of import-competing products. These changes in prices translate into changes in factor rewards that benefit the export-allied inputs and hurt the import-allied inputs.

The impact of trade on income distribution in a framework that emphasizes sectoral affinities of inputs, but that is more flexible than our example, was developed by Jones (1971). Imagine an economy that produces cloth and wine with constant returns to scale (i.e., the technologies have the property that a proportional increase in all inputs raises output by the same factor of proportionality), in which cloth is produced with capital (machines) and labor, while wine is produced with land and labor. As in Ricardo's example, labor is homogeneous (there are no wine or cloth specialists), and workers move freely across sectors. When this type of economy opens to foreign trade, it may end up exporting cloth or wine. If it exports cloth, the owners of capital benefit from trade while the owners of land lose. The workers may gain or lose in welfare terms, because trade raises their wine-wage and reduces their cloth-wage. Under the circumstances the workers gain if they drink a lot of wine and consume little cloth, but they lose if their spending pattern is biased toward cloth. Unlike the previous example, however, now the wage is not fixed in terms of either wine or cloth; it changes in terms of both goods when trade opens up. And the same applies to the rewards of the other factors of production, which are trapped in their respective sectors. Similar conclusions emerge when the country exports wine, except that in this case land-owners benefit while capital owners lose. The general conclusion is that the sector-specific input that is allied with the export sector gains from trade while the sector-specific input that is allied with the import-competing sector loses. The footloose input, labor, which is allied with neither sector, may gain or lose.

So far I have used an extreme notion of sectoral alliances of inputs; an input is allied with a sector if it is employable in this sector but *not* employable in any other industry. The lack of employability in other sectors can arise for at least two reasons: first, because the technology in the other sectors is designed to use different inputs; and second, because the input cannot be reallocated to other uses. In either case, sectoral specificity occurs. A prevalent view is that some specificity arises in the short run because of the difficulty of quickly and costlessly reallocating inputs across industries, but that factors of production can be productively redeployed across sectors in the long run (see Mussa, 1974, and Neary, 1978). For this reason it is interesting to study economies in which all factors of production can be productively employed in all industries. The conclusions from such an investigation can then be interpreted as pertaining to long-run outcomes.

Be this as it may, does the notion of sectoral affinity of inputs lose its usefulness when factors of production move freely across industries? The answer is no, except that the nature of this alliance is different. To illustrate, consider a two-sector two-factor economy of the type we examined in the previous chapter when discussing the factor proportions theory. For concreteness, suppose that cloth and wine are produced with labor and capital under constant returns to scale, that cloth is capital-intensive and wine is labor-intensive, and that both capital and labor move freely across these industries. If England exports cloth, this means that the relative price of cloth is higher in the trade regime than it was in England in autarky. What does this imply about the gains from trade for workers and capital owners? The answer is provided by Stolper and Samuelson (1941). They show that an increase in the price of a product raises by a larger percentage the reward of the input used intensively in its production, and reduces the reward of the other input. As a consequence, the real income of the former input rises (because this income can now buy more of both goods) while the real income of the latter input falls (because the purchasing power of this factor's reward is now lower in terms of both goods). This implies that in England capital owners gain from trade while workers lose. In terms of sectoral alliances, we can think about capital as allied with the export industry—which is intensive in capital—and about labor as allied with the import-competing industry—which is intensive in labor.

Mayda and Rodrik (2005) find empirical support for both notions of sectoral alliance in their study of individual attitudes toward trade. First, individuals with high levels of human capital, measured either by education or occupational categories, tend to oppose trade restrictions in countries with large endowments of human capital but not in countries with low endowments. The interpretation is that in countries with large endowments of human capital, highly educated and highly skilled individuals are expected to gain from freer trade, which raises export prices relative to import prices, because exports of these countries are human capital–intensive. In contrast, in countries with low endowments of human capital, highly educated and skilled individuals gain from high prices of imports, because in these countries the import-competing sectors are human capital–intensive. Second, individuals support or oppose trade restrictions on the basis of sectoral affiliations. In particular, those who work in nontraded sectors have protrade preferences while those who work in sectors with a revealed comparative disadvantage have the strongest antitrade biases. The interpretation is that factor rewards are sector specific. On the one hand, the real income of a factor is higher when its sector of employment sells products for higher prices, and for this reason individuals working in export sectors (with revealed comparative advantage)—which have higher prices under trade—oppose trade restrictions. On the other hand, individuals working in nontraded sectors benefit from trade as a result of low import prices, and therefore they too oppose trade restrictions.

We have examined in some detail the impact of trade on factor rewards in small-scale models (i.e., models with a small number of industries and a small number of inputs), which illustrate mechanisms of transmission from commodity prices to factor rewards. These small-scale models yield sharp predictions. The question is which of these predictions generalize to more complex environments, with many goods and many factors of production. Jones and Scheinkman (1977) provide an answer. They show that in an economy that produces all goods with constant returns to scale, an increase in the price of a product raises at least one factor reward proportionately more and reduces at least one factor reward.[64] Naturally, a factor of production whose reward rises proportionately more than the price increase gains from the price hike, while a factor of production whose reward declines loses. This means that every price increase benefits some factors of production and hurts others. Since international trade raises prices of exportables relative to import-competing products, trade is bound to impact the functional distribution of income (i.e., the income of different factors of production). In the process, some gain while others lose.

When trade benefits some individuals and hurts others, the interesting question is whether the gainers can compensate the losers. My discussion abstracted from the possibility of government-mandated income redistribution in response to trade. But one can ask, "Can governments redistribute income in a way that ensures gains from trade for all?" This question is addressed in the next section.

3.4 Compensating Losers

In neoclassical economies with diminishing marginal productivity of inputs and price-taking in all markets, international trade expands every country's consumption opportunities. This observation goes back to Samuelson (1939), who studied a small price-taking country, and Kemp (1962) and Samuelson (1962), who extended Samuelson's original insights to large countries.[65] But, as we have seen in the previous section, better consumption opportunities for a country do not necessarily translate into better consumption opportunities for all its residents. A government can step in under these circumstances and use its taxing power to shift income from individuals who gain from trade to those who might lose, in order to effect a more equitable distribution of these gains. Naturally, whether such a strategy can secure gains from trade for all depends on the policy instruments available for this purpose. The best-case scenario for the realization of such broad-based gains from trade arises when the government can use lump-sum taxes and subsidies, targeted at individuals or households. These taxes and subsidies are levied independently of a person's activities, so that the person cannot change the tax liability or subsidy payout by changing behavior. The reason is that, on the one hand, lump-sum redistributive instruments do not impose *economic inefficiencies,* and therefore do not reduce the size of the "pie" available for redistribution, and on the other hand, such instruments do not limit the extent of *feasible* redistributions, because they enable the government to shift income across individuals as much or as little as it wants. True, such instruments are hardly ever available in practice (a poll tax being the exception), but they provide an important analytical benchmark for understanding the issues at hand. I therefore begin the discussion with lump-sum redistribution and proceed to examine other types of taxes and subsidies afterward.

The general result is that in neoclassical economies every country can find a lump-sum redistribution scheme that ensures gains from trade for all its residents. Before explaining the logic of this remarkable result, let me illustrate it with the example of cloth and wine specialists from the previous section.

Suppose that in England the cloth specialists produce 100 units of cloth and the wine specialists produce 100 units of wine. In autarky a unit of cloth is 50 percent more expensive than a unit of wine. Table 3.1 describes the autarky trade of goods between these two groups of specialists; the cloth specialists sell 40 units of cloth and buy 60 units of wine, while the wine specialists sell 60 units of wine and buy 40 units of cloth.

Table 3.1.   Autarky Equilibrium with an Output of 100 Units of Cloth and
               100 Units of Wine

	Cloth Specialists			Wine Specialists		
	Sell	Buy	Consume	Sell	Buy	Consume
Cloth	40	0	60	0	40	40
Wine	0	60	60	60	0	40

The relative price is 1.5 units of wine for a unit of cloth. Under these circumstances cloth specialists consume 60 units of cloth and 60 units of wine, while the wine specialists consume 40 units of cloth and 40 units of wine.

Next consider a trading regime in which the price of cloth is 40 percent higher than the price of wine. As explained in the previous section, under this price configuration and without income redistribution, the wine specialists gain and the cloth specialists lose from trade. To see how every group can be made better off in a trading regime than in autarky, consider lump-sum redistribution. In particular, consider a lump-sum tax on wine specialists equal in value to 4 units of wine, and a lump-sum transfer to cloth specialists also equal in value to 4 units of wine. Moreover, the same tax applies to every wine specialist and the same subsidy applies to every cloth specialist. From the point of view of the government, this is a feasible policy, because it is budget-balanced; the tax revenue just equals the subsidy bill. With this fiscal scheme in place, the cloth specialists can still consume 60 units of cloth and 60 units of wine, and the wine specialists can still consume 40 units of cloth and 40 units of wine. The reason is that if the cloth specialists sell 40 units of cloth, as they did in autarky, they are able to purchase with the proceeds from this sale $1.4 \times 40 = 56$ units of wine, and they can buy an additional 4 units of wine with the lump-sum subsidy. In this way they can consume 60 units of wine. In addition, they can consume the 60 units of cloth that remain in their possession. As for the wine specialists, they can sell 4 units of wine in order to pay the lump-sum tax, and sell in addition 56 units of wine in order to use the proceeds to purchase cloth. This leaves them with 40 units of wine for consumption. The proceeds from the 56 units of wine can then be used to purchase 40 units of cloth (56 ÷ 1.4), which allows the wine specialists to consume the autarky amounts of cloth and wine.

Evidently, if the cloth and wine specialists were to respond to the lump-sum taxes and subsidies so as to preserve their autarky consumption levels, they would be as well off in the trading equilibrium as they were in autarky. However, the key to the gains from trade is that they can do better than this. The reason is that by facing the autarky relative price of 1.5 units of wine per unit of cloth, the cloth specialists and the wine specialists have chosen to consume 60-60 and 40-40 units, respectively, and this is in each case the best mix of consumption for the given relative price. Therefore, with the relative price of cloth falling to 1.4, it is quite unlikely that the equal mixes will remain the best consumption compositions. In particular, given that the 60-60 and 40-40 compositions are still feasible, every person should strictly prefer to cut back on wine consumption and raise the consumption of cloth as compared to his autarky choice, because cloth is now relatively cheaper. In other words, although the autarky consumption levels are feasible for every person, the new prices and income allow him to choose a better consumption mix. As a result, the proposed redistribution scheme secures gains from trade for everyone.[66]

The structure of the argument from this example applies more generally when there are many different people with different sources of income, many types of inputs and final products, and more complex technologies. It proceeds as follows. Let the government construct lump-sum taxes and subsidies that ensure that every individual's income in the trading equilibrium is just sufficient to purchase his autarky consumption bundle. Then, from the fact that autarky relative prices of consumption goods differ from the relative prices in the trading equilibrium, it follows that by moving from autarky to the trade regime every individual can reconfigure his spending pattern beneficially so as to increase consumption of the cheaper goods in the trade regime and reduce consumption of the more expensive goods. The only question that arises is whether the proposed lump-sum redistribution scheme is feasible, in the sense that it does not generate a budget deficit. Because if it were to generate a budget deficit, it would imply that the economy's aggregate spending exceeds its income. Fortunately, this policy generates a budget surplus.[67] For this reason, the government can in fact use higher transfers or lower taxes to achieve budget balance, and therefore benefit some individuals even more. In other words, the government can ensure gains from trade for all.

Lump-sum taxes and subsidies are difficult to use, and especially so when they need to be finely targeted at specific individuals, because they require enormous amounts of information that is impossible to obtain. For example, in the redistribution policy just proposed, the government needs to know the value of every individual's consumption level in autarky, data that are hardly ever available. For this reason one might ask whether other types of policies, which do not require information about individuals but rather information about market outcomes, can also be used to secure gains from trade for all. The answer, provided by Dixit and Norman (1986), is that such policies do exist. Dixit and Norman propose the following policy scheme: let the government of a country tax or subsidize products and inputs in the trading regime so as to ensure that the prices of goods and factor rewards faced by the country's residents are the same in the trading regime as they were in autarky. Note that this policy does not require the government to know who consumes what or what the sources of individual incomes are; to design this policy the government experts need to use market-generated information only. In other words, this policy design preserves individual anonymity, in the sense that it treats individuals equally with market-driven variables. With this policy in place, every individual faces in the trading equilibrium the same opportunities and tradeoff as in autarky, and therefore every individual ends up choosing the autarky consumption mix that yields the autarky welfare level. In other words, under this policy every individual is equally well off in the trade regime as in autarky. What Dixit and Norman then show is that this policy generates a budget surplus. It therefore follows that the government can reduce prices of some goods that everyone consumes, such as certain food items, in order to reach budget balance. These lower prices lead every individual to reconfigure his consumption in a way that makes him better off. Therefore, all individuals gain from trade.

The Dixit-Norman policy design involves substantial distortions, which shrink the "pie" available for distribution. Nevertheless, the smaller pie is sufficiently large to give everyone a larger slice than in autarky. Unfortunately, as beautiful as this result is, it does not offer a practical way for designing policies that ensure broad-based gains from trade. Moreover, even if one could identify practical policies of this sort, it would be difficult to secure their implementation in representative democracies or autocratic regimes, in which interest groups play a major role in policy formation (see Grossman and Helpman, 2002b). For this reason, conflicts of interest over trade policies remain prevalent.

4

Scale and Scope

Traditional approaches to comparative advantage focus on industries as units of observation, and these in practice are represented by more or less disaggregated data sets. An underlying rationale behind this approach is that in every industry outputs of different firms are highly substitutable for each other, and so there is no harm in assuming that a sector supplies a homogeneous product. In this view Italian tiles from Modena are nearly perfect substitutes for Israeli tiles from Jerusalem, and Pierre Cardin shirts for men are nearly perfect substitutes for Van Heusen shirts for men. In other words, although tiles and shirts come in different brands, we can understand which country has a comparative advantage in tiles and which has a comparative advantage in shirts without accounting for product differentiation within sectors. Indeed, we have seen in Chapter 2 that this approach can take us a long way in understanding sectoral trade patterns as resulting from productivity differences and differences in factor composition across countries.

Nevertheless, some features of trade data are at odds with this view. First, whereas models that emphasize differences in country characteristics as the source of trade predict large trade flows between countries with different productivities and factor endowments and small trade flows between countries with similar productivities and factor endowments, the trade data reveal large trade flows across countries with similar characteristics. Second, the majority of trade is not across sectors but rather within industries. That is, instead of observing a country that exports tiles to import shirts, we observe a country that exports tiles to also import tiles, and we observe the same country to export and import shirts. While differences in productivity and factor endowments can help explain why such a country may export tiles on net and import shirts on net, they fail to explain why such a country also imports tiles and exports shirts.

To illustrate these features, first consider the regional structure of trade in manufactures in 2005, as depicted in Table 4.1. Exports totaled over $10 trillion ($10,159 billion). Of these, about 15 percent originated in North America and about 43 percent originated in Europe. The rest, about 42 percent of world exports, originated in other regions of the world (South and Central America, Africa, Asia, the Middle East). In addition, about 21 percent of world exports were destined for North America and 43 percent for Europe. The residual, about 36 percent, were destined for other regions of the world. Importantly, exports from rich countries in Europe and North America to other rich countries in Europe and North America accounted for about 46 percent of world trade. Adding Japanese trade with Europe and North America raises the share of rich countries in world trade to 50 percent. In other words, trade

Table 4.1. Regional Structure of Exports of Manufactures, 2005

Origin\Destination	North America	Europe	Japan	World
North America	824	238	88	1478
Europe	398	3201	77	4372
Japan	152	94	0	595
World	2093	4398	515	10159

Source: World Trade Organization (2006, table 3.3 and table 3.70), in billions of U.S. dollars.

among a handful of the richest countries accounts for half the volume of world trade. This concentration of trade among rich countries that are more similar to each other in terms of productivity and factor endowments than they are to poorer countries in Asia, Africa, or South America does not square well with the traditional views of comparative advantage.

Next consider trade within industries. Grubel and Lloyd (1975) developed an index, now known as the Grubel-Lloyd Index, for measuring the fraction of trade flows that take place within industries as opposed to across sectors. Using this decomposition they showed that in many countries the majority of trade is intra-industry rather than intersectoral. Table 4.2 shows average shares of intra-industry trade in a sample of countries for the years 1996–2000. France has the highest share; more than three-quarters of its trade is intra-industry and less than a quarter is intersectoral. Australia, on the other hand, has the lowest share; less than 30 percent of its trade is intra-industry and more than 70 percent is

Table 4.2.   Shares of Intra-industry Trade (in Percent), 1996–2000 Average

France	77.5
Czech Republic	77.4
Canada	76.2
United Kingdom	73.7
Mexico	73.4
Hungary	72.1
Germany	72.0
Spain	71.2
Netherlands	68.9
United States	68.5
Sweden	66.6
Italy	64.7
Korea	57.5
Japan	47.6
New Zealand	40.6
Norway	37.1
Australia	29.8

Source: Organisation for Economic Co-operation and Development (2002, table 6.1).

intersectoral. It is evident from this table that countries at different levels of development—such as Canada and the United Kingdom, on the one hand, and the Czech Republic and Hungary, on the other—have shares of intra-industry trade that are very high indeed.

Shares of intra-industry trade vary not only across countries, but also across industries. In the United States, for example, inorganic chemicals, power-generating machinery, and electrical machinery all had shares of intra-industry trade in excess of 95 percent in 1993. On the other side, iron and steel had a share of 43 percent and clothing and apparel had a share of 27 percent (see Krugman and Obstfeld, 2009, table 6-3).

How can we explain these patterns? For this purpose it helps to think about product differentiation within industries. If Italian tiles from Modena are not perfect substitutes for Israeli tiles from Jerusalem, then Italy can export tiles to Israel and Israel can export tiles to Italy. And if electrical machinery manufactured in the United States differs from electrical machinery manufactured in Germany, then the United States can import electrical machinery from Germany and Germany can import electrical machinery from the United States.

Once product differentiation is recognized as a cause of trade flows, it helps explain the fact that a large part of the observed variation in trade represents variation in the number of traded products rather than in quantities per product. Hummels and Klenow (2005) show that about 60 percent of the differences in trade values across countries of different size—with larger countries exporting more than smaller countries—are explained by the *extensive margin* of trade. That is, larger countries export a wider range of products than smaller countries. Figure 4.1 depicts the relationship between country size and the extensive margin of trade; it shows clearly that larger countries, as measured by GDP, export a wider range of products.[68]

Although international trade in differentiated products had been an important phenomenon for many years, it was integrated into trade theory only in the 1980s.[69] That was when economists found ways to formally

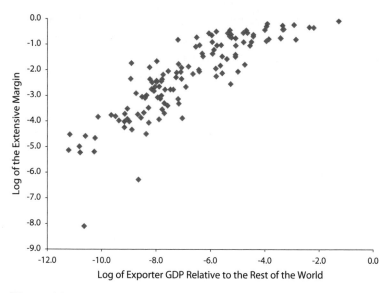

Figure 4.1. Variation in the range of traded products, 126 countries. Data from Hummels and Klenow (2005).

model markets in which firms operate under economies of scale and specialize in different brands of various products. Because economies of scale play a role distinct from product differentiation, I will discuss the impact on trade of economies of scale *without* product differentiation in the next section, and *with* product differentiation in the section that follows.

4.1 Economies of Scale

Economies of scale can arise in different ways, but the two most commonly encountered forms originate in technology and agglomeration. In this section we deal with technology-driven economies of scale, the idea being that certain production processes have the property that a proportional expansion of all input use raises output more than proportionately.

As an example, consider the manufacturing of tiles. If by raising the use of clay, of machinery and equipment, of structures and labor by, say, 10 percent, the output of tiles were to go up by more than 10 percent, we would say that the technology for manufacturing tiles exhibits increasing returns to scale, or just economies of scale. If, on the other hand, the expansion of input use by 10 percent were to raise output by less than 10 percent, we would say that the technology exhibits diminishing returns to scale. And if the expansion of input use by 10 percent were to raise output by exactly 10 percent, we would say that the technology exhibits constant returns to scale. More accurately, a technology exhibits economies of scale if *every* proportional expansion of input use raises output more than proportionally, and similarly for diminishing and constant returns to scale. That is, to qualify for one of the three classifications, the property has to be satisfied for *every* proportional expansion of input use.[70] Importantly, economies of scale lead to declining average costs. That is, average costs are lower the larger the output level, while decreasing returns to scale lead to rising average costs. Average costs are constant when the returns to scale are constant.

Scale economies are common in sectors with significant fixed costs, such as aircraft and pharmaceuticals. These fixed costs can arise from either development costs or setup costs of production lines. In aircraft, for example, the development of a model, such as a wide-bodied jet, is very expensive, and so is the construction of a manufacturing line for a specific model. In pharmaceuticals, the development of a drug can be notoriously expensive, running to hundreds of millions of dollars. In either case there are economies of scale. For other products, fixed costs can be much lower, creating economies of scale nevertheless.

To illustrate how fixed costs generate economies of scale, consider a simple example in which a carpenter manufactures tables in his own shop, so that all inputs consist of materials and his working hours.[71] To produce a table of a certain kind, say a square kitchen table of size 2×2 yards, the carpenter has to spend four hours thinking about the design and the stages of production: which parts to prepare first, which to glue, which to bolt, and the like. Once these details have been sorted out, it takes him two hours to produce a table. So it may appear that the carpenter's production process exhibits constant returns to scale, because by doubling his *construction* hours and *materials*—such as timber, glue, and bolts—he will produce double the number of tables. Yet this disregards the four hours it took him to think through the design and the stages of production. These four hours are needed only once, independently of how many tables he produces. Therefore by doubling the number of working hours and materials, the carpenter more than doubles the number of hours actually devoted to the construction of tables, and can therefore more than double the number of tables he produces. The principles embodied in this example apply naturally to much more complex manufacturing processes.

My discussion in the previous two chapters assumed that technologies exhibit constant returns to scale. Under this assumption we examined the structure of trade and its impact on income distribution for economies with competitive markets. The resulting patterns of specialization were determined by differences in technologies or differences in factor endowments across countries. However, prominent scholars—such as Graham (1923) and Ohlin (1933)—pointed out many years ago that economies of scale can be an independent source of specialization, and therefore can impact the structure of foreign trade. A country that manages to attain large-scale production in an industry with economies of scale manufactures its product with low unit cost and therefore exports this product. That is, scale of production is a source of comparative advantage. Under these circumstances the concentration of production in a few countries—or, even better, in one country—attains large-scale production and low unit cost, reducing prices for all buyers around the world. As a result, there is a presumption that increasing returns render an independent source of gains from trade, and that this adds to the gains from differences in prices between trade and autarky that were discussed in the previous chapter.

However, Graham (1923) was concerned with the possibility that a country might be hurt by foreign trade when some of its production activities are subject to increasing returns to scale, and that such a country might be better off protecting its import-competing sectors. He reasoned as follows. Suppose that there are two industries, one operating under constant returns to scale, the other under increasing returns to scale, and suppose that when trade opens up resources flow from the increasing- to the constant-returns sector. Then productivity (output per unit input) declines in the former sector and remains flat in the latter, leading to a fall in the value of GDP at constant prices and possibly to a decline in welfare. If the sector with economies of scale competes with imports, tariff protection can prevent the reallocation of inputs to the constant-returns-to-scale sector and thereby prevent a contraction of GDP.

Knight (1924) criticized Graham's argument, pointing out that it is not possible to apply standard competitive analysis to situations with increasing returns. The debate between these scholars was important, because it brought to the fore noteworthy considerations concerning the operation of markets with increasing returns. Are the scale economies internal to the firm? That is, does a proportional expansion of the firm's inputs raise the firm's output more than proportionately? Are they internal to a country's industry or to the world's industry? That is, does a country's output of, say, chemicals rise more than proportionately when the country's chemical industry expands proportionately all its inputs, or does the world's chemical industry expand output more than proportionately when the world's chemical industry expands inputs proportionately? Can such markets be competitive? Are prices driven by marginal or average costs in these types of industries? After discussing the debate between Graham and Knight in his exhaustive review of scholarly work on international trade, Jacob Viner summarized his position thus:

A conceivable case for protection on the basis of the existence of external economies in an industry which from the individual producer's point of view is at a comparative disadvantage in costs can be made out, therefore, only where these external economies are (a) dependent on the size of the national and not the world industry and (b) are technological rather than pecuniary, or, if pecuniary, are not at the expense of domestic sellers of services or materials to the industry. The scope for the application of the argument is extremely limited, especially as it seems difficult even to suggest plausible hypothetical cases of the existence of genuine technological external economies. Instead of providing a substantial "scientific" basis for the popularity of protection among the vulgar, as Graham seems to think, his thesis reduces to little more than a theoretical curiosity. (Viner, 1965, pp. 480–481, original edition, 1937)

Indeed, Graham's conjecture is easiest to support when economies of scale are external to the firm and internal to the industry, in the sense suggested by Marshall (1920, Book 4, chapters 9–11). That is, the productivity of a firm in the import-competing sector depends on the sector's domestic output—the larger the industry is, the more efficient every firm is—yet a single manufacturer takes as given the industry's size, and therefore views his productivity as being independent of his own deployment of inputs. Under these circumstances individual manufacturers operate under the perception of constant returns to scale while their sector exhibits increasing returns. In this case all manufacturers can be price takers and the competitive paradigm can be preserved.

Ethier (1982a) formalized this intuition and showed that Graham was right, in the sense that in some circumstances trade leads to the contraction of a country's increasing-returns import-competing sector and to welfare losses from trade, in which case protection is beneficial. Importantly, however, contraction of a country's increasing-returns import-competing sector does not lead *necessarily* to losses from trade, because the sources of gains from trade that we discussed in Chapter 3 still operate. In other words, now some economic forces make international trade gainful and others make it detrimental. On net, there can be gains or losses from trade.[72]

Economies of scale introduce a certain degree of arbitrariness into the pattern of trade, because a country that produces a large volume of output in an increasing-returns sector gains a cost advantage in this sector as a result of the affinity between high output and high productivity in this sort of industry. In other words, there is an interesting circularity in this environment: while high productivity leads to high output (as, for example, in Ricardo's world), now high output leads also to high productivity. As a result, a country that happens to produce a large volume of output ends up with high productivity and a low unit cost, while a country that happens to produce a small volume of output ends up with low productivity and a high unit cost. Under these circumstances the country that happens to produce the larger volume becomes an exporter while the country that happens to produce the smaller volume becomes an importer. Yet the roles of these countries can be reversed, with the former producing a small volume and the latter producing a large volume, because both a large and a small volume of output are self-sustaining. And naturally, reversing the pattern of specialization reverses the direction of trade. The point is that a country needs no special characteristics to gain a comparative advantage in a sector of this type, so that either one of the countries can become the larger producer and thus the exporter of the product. This property leads to multiple equilibria, making it difficult to predict the patterns of specialization and trade.

An interesting commentary on this lack of predictability is provided by Grossman and Rossi-Hansberg (2010). They point out that the multiplicity of equilibria in a Graham-Ethier-type world is driven by the combination of two assumptions: industries are large in terms of resource use, and firms are price takers. In cases in which industries are small, firms do not take productivity as given but instead recognize that it rises with size, firms recognize their ability to exercise market power and take as given pricing strategies of rival manufacturers, then predictable trade patterns are restored by Ricardian forces of comparative advantage, as in Dornbusch, Fischer, and Samuelson (1977). In the Grossman–Rossi-Hansberg world there are many tiny industries and two trading countries whose comparative costs are determined by relative productivity differences, as in Dornbusch, Fischer, and Samuelson. Unlike Dornbusch, Fischer, and Samuelson, however, the labor requirement per unit output falls with a country's output level, and this scale effect—which is country specific—is the same in both countries. Firms compete in prices: every firm chooses its price, taking as given the prices of its rivals, and it accommodates the quantity demanded for its product at these prices. Since goods are homogeneous, the demand faced by a firm collapses to zero if it charges a price that exceeds the price of any other firm in the industry. As a result, only the lowest-price firms can sell their products. Moreover, active firms have to at least cover their costs, and therefore their price cannot fall short of the average cost. Therefore every active firm charges a price that just equals its average cost.[73] In this type of highly contestable market, specialization and trade are governed by Ricardian forces of comparative advantage.[74]

Evidently, Grossman and Rossi-Hansberg depart from competitive behavior by firms; their firms do not take the market prices as given. Departures from competitive behavior are in fact a necessary feature of industries with economies of scale, in which every firm recognizes that its unit cost declines with output expansion. The reason is that in such industries firms have market power, they can be large, and they behave strategically, exploiting their market power. The precise nature of the resulting market outcome depends then on these strategies, which take different forms in different industries. As a result, an analysis of industries with returns to scale cannot be divorced from a sector's market structure and its firms' conduct.

Are economies of scale a mere curiosity? Or can they be found in weighty sectors? Empirical estimates of production functions find significant economies of scale in some sectors, such as railroads and electric power generation.[75] Other sectors appear to have constant returns to scale. Antweiler and Trefler (2002) use Vanek's approach to the factor content of trade flows (discussed in Chapter 2) to estimate sectoral economies of scale from trade data. Instead of allowing productivity to differ across countries either in a Hicks-neutral or in a factor-augmenting fashion, as in Trefler (1993, 1995), they assume that productivity varies with an industry's scale and that this relationship can be approximated with a power function (i.e., productivity equals output raised to some positive power). In this event, the parameter of the power function can be estimated from the data. They find that many traditional sectors—such as apparel, leather, footwear, and textiles—exhibit constant returns to scale. A number of natural resource sectors—such as livestock and coal mining—exhibit small economies of scale, while forestry exhibits larger economies of scale. Among the manufacturing industries, petroleum and coal products and pharmaceuticals exhibit large economies of scale; electric and electronic machinery and petroleum refineries exhibit intermediate economies of scale, similar in size to forestry; and instruments and nonelectric machinery exhibit substantial, although smaller, economies of scale.[76] In view of these findings it would be inappropriate to marginalize economies of scale in the analysis of trade flows; countries that manage to build up large-scale activities in increasing-returns sectors gain cost advantages in these industries and export their products.[77]

However, in many industries the scale economies are not external to the firm. In this event firms are not price takers, and it is necessary to explicitly consider noncompetitive conduct. For this reason we discuss monopolistic competition in the next section.[78]

4.2 Monopolistic Competition

Most products come in an assortment of varieties; there are many brands of cheese and wine, shirts and suits. Refrigerators, washing machines,

and vacuum cleaners all come in many varieties, as do hairstyling estab-
lishments, restaurants, and dental clinics. In both manufacturing and
service sectors, suppliers gain from differentiating their products from
those offered by competitors, and this creates strong incentives to invest
in branding. Investment in product differentiation generates in turn
economies of scale at the firm (or product) level. A company that develops a particular brand of a product, such as a special flavor of ice cream
or a unique cellular telephone, bears this investment cost independently
of whether its sales are large or small. Naturally, the decision to invest
depends on expected sales, but once the investment bears fruit the company can manufacture many units or few units, regardless of the investment that has been sunk. These fixed costs lead to economies of scale.[79]

In sectors with product differentiation and firm-specific economies of
scale, firms need to make profits after entry in order to cover their entry
costs. For this they need to exercise market power. If, for example, product development requires investment but any other firm could costlessly
learn the technology for manufacturing a brand developed by a rival firm
and sell its product as a perfect substitute for the product of the original
developer, then this would diminish the incentive to develop new products and possibly eliminate such incentives altogether. For this reason
some degree of market power is required to encourage entry of multiple
brands. This type of market power is acquired naturally if a brand of a
product produced by one firm is perceived to be an imperfect substitute
for other brands of the same product.

If product differentiation did not entail fixed costs, then firms would
secure the supply of every conceivable brand that is demanded by consumers or firms. In other words, products would be tailor-made for every
taste and need. But this is obviously not the case in practice; there is
limited variety available in the marketplace, and buyers choose which
brands suit them best at the going prices. Economies of scale at the
brand level secure a limited supply of brands. And entry of new manufacturers exerts competitive pressure on the firms in an industry. This is

what defines monopolistic competition. Although every firm has market power, in the sense that by reducing the price of its brand it can sell more, in equilibrium this market power does not translate into positive profits because entry of rival firms ensures that overall profits—accounting for the fixed costs of product development and the setting up of shop in the industry—equal zero.

In many cases the legal system protects product developers, either through patents or brand names. To illustrate the former, consider pharmaceutical products. In the United States brand-name drugs are protected by patent for 20 years. When a patent expires, other drug manufacturers can be authorized to produce generic substitutes. The website of the Food and Drug Administration (FDA) explains that "a generic drug is a copy that is the same as a brand-name drug in dosage, safety, strength, how it is taken, quality, performance and intended use." And it also explains that "generic drugs are less expensive because generic manufacturers don't have the investment costs of the developer of a new drug. New drugs are developed under patent protection. The patent protects the investment—including research, development, marketing, and promotion—by giving the company the sole right to sell the drug while it is in effect."[80] Nevertheless, generic drugs coexist with brand-name products, despite the fact that the generic drugs are much cheaper. Evidently, consumers do not perceive the generics to be perfect substitutes for brand-name products.

To illustrate the latter, note that registered brand names are also protected. As a result, neither Levi's jeans nor shoes with Adidas labels can be produced and marketed by unauthorized companies. That is, the legal system gives brand names monopoly power.

Brand names can also be maintained with little or no legal protection. While I cannot open an unauthorized McDonald's hamburger outlet, I can open a hamburger store under my own label and sell a product with unique characteristics that hamburger lovers appreciate. The success of my enterprise will depend on how many people find my hamburgers and their prices attractive. As long as other hamburger sellers cannot replicate the characteristics of my product, I can exercise some degree of monopoly power, in the sense that—within a range—my sales rise in response to my lowering of prices.

Edward Chamberlin (1933) developed an analytical framework for handling this type of situation. Particularly useful has proved to be his "large group" case, which applies to an industry in which the economies of scale at the firm level are small relative to the demand for the sector's products, so that many firms with different brands can profitably enter the industry. As a result, firms enter up to the point at which the profits of incumbents are close to zero and no incentive exists for additional firms to enter. Since every manufacturer exercises some monopoly power, with this power being limited by the number of competitors and the degree to which their products substitute well for his, the manufacturer prices his brand above the marginal cost of production to maximize profits. The resulting markup of price above marginal cost generates operating profits, but these profits are just sufficient to cover the entry cost, in which case overall profits are close to zero.

This outcome, which is reflective of Chamberlin-style monopolistic competition, is illustrated in Figure 4.2. The output of a representative firm is measured on the horizontal axis and its price and average cost are measured on the vertical axis. The figure depicts the firm's demand curve and average cost curve, showing how price and average cost decline with output. At point A, the two curves are tangent to each other. This means that if the firm manufactures the output corresponding to point A, it sells this output at a price that equals average cost and its overall profits equal zero. If, instead, the firm produces less than this output level, average cost exceeds the price, yielding negative profits. And similarly, if the firm produces more than this output level, average cost also exceeds the price, yielding negative profits. In other words, the firm breaks even when it manufactures an output level corresponding to point A and loses money at all other output levels. Therefore A is the equilibrium point.

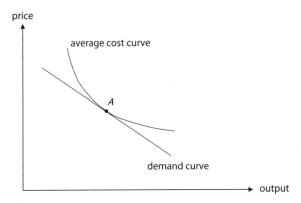

Figure 4.2. Monopolistic competition: output and price.

How is the tangency point *A* attained? One important mechanism emphasized by Chamberlin is entry and exit of firms. If, for example, the demand curve in Figure 4.2 were higher, then at some output levels the price would be above average cost, in which case profits would be positive. Such profits attract new firms to enter the industry. As new firms enter, the demand facing an incumbent falls because of the availability of more substitutes for the incumbent's brand. If, alternatively, the demand curve were lower in Figure 4.2, an incumbent would lose money no matter how much he were to produce. As a result, firms exit. The exit of firms induces an upward shift in the demand curve of every remaining firm in the industry. At the end, a tangency—similar to point *A*—characterizes every active firm.

The logic of monopolistic competition works equally well in economies engaged in foreign trade as in economies not engaged in foreign trade. The difference is that if an economy is isolated from the rest of the world, a manufacturer of one of its differentiated products will make sure that her brand differs from other brands produced in her economy, but she will not care whether her brand differs from brands available in other countries. On the other hand, if the economy trades with other countries, then each one of its manufacturers will make sure that her brand differs from every brand supplied in the world economy, that is, in her own country as well as in every other country. In other words, trade leads to competitive product differentiation across the globe rather than only within countries. This is good news for consumers who value variety, because trade affords them access to a wider variety choice. When my country trades with other countries, I can choose to purchase a domestic brand of a washing machine or a foreign brand, whichever better fits my budget and my needs. And this additional variety choice proves to be an important source of gains from trade.

To gauge the importance of imported varieties, consider the U.S. economy. Between 1972 and 1988, the number of imported brands increased by 119 percent, while between 1990 and 2001 this number increased by 42 percent. This means that during the entire period, imported variety rose by 212 percent.[81] As Broda and Weinstein (2006, pp. 552–553) point out, about half of this increase was due to a rise in the number of goods and about half due to a rise in the number of countries exporting each good to the United States. As a result, between 1972 and 2001 the growth of variety has contributed a 28 percent decline in the variety-adjusted import price index and a 2.6 percent gain in real income.[82] Evidently, growth in imported variety had a significant effect on the U.S. economy.

International exchange of differentiated products predicts trade flows that differ in important ways from international exchange of homogeneous goods. In addition to predicting intra-industry trade, trade in differentiated products predicts trade volumes that respond differently to country characteristics than trade in homogeneous goods. A key difference concerns factor endowments. In a Heckscher-Ohlin world, in which differences in factor composition across countries feed foreign trade, we expect trade volumes to be large across countries with large differences in factor composition and small across countries with small differences in factor composition. In the data, however, this is not the case. As already illustrated, the largest trade flows take place across the industrial countries, which have similar factor compositions, and little trade takes place between the industrial and less-developed countries, which differ greatly in factor composition. This is not to say that differences in factor composition do not impact trade flows—they do—but rather to say that in order to understand foreign trade we need to understand additional determinants of trade flows.

Tinbergen (1962) suggested an empirical approach to trade flows, using what is known as the "gravity equation." In physics, the gravitational pull between two particles of matter is directly proportional to the product of their masses and inversely proportional to the square of the distance between them. In Tinbergen's specification, the trade volume between a pair of countries is proportional to the product of their market sizes, as measured by the GDP of each country (the gravity component, analogous to the product of masses). The factor of proportionality differs across country pairs according to impediments to their bilateral trade flows (the trade-resistance measure, analogous to the square of distance). These impediments may result from natural factors, such as distance between the countries that impacts shipment costs, or man-made impediments, such as tariffs. But other factors, such as whether they share a common language, may also influence the trade-resistance measure. Tinbergen's approach has been applied to many data sets and has withstood the test of time. It works surprisingly well in explaining trade flows across countries at different levels of development and in different periods.

While a Tinbergen-style gravity equation does not arise naturally from the traditional factor proportions approach to foreign trade, it does arise naturally when this approach is augmented to include product differentiation.[83] As Helpman (1987) points out, in the extreme case of product differentiation in all sectors, trade flows obey an exact gravity equation.[84] The reason is that under these circumstances every country specializes in different brands of every product, so that suppliers from one country offer brands distinct from those of other countries. As a result, in every country demand exists for all the brands produced in the world economy. In the absence of trade impediments and with similar homothetic preferences in all countries, a country's demand for every brand is proportional to its size. This means that if a country's size is, say, 5 percent of the world's economy, it demands 5 percent of every brand, in which case it imports 5 percent of the GDP of each one of its trade partners. Similarly, a trade partner whose size is, say, 10 percent of the world's economy, imports 10 percent of each country's GDP. For this reason the trade flows between the two countries consist of 5 percent of the latter country's GDP plus 10 percent of the former country's GDP. But since the former country's GDP is 5 percent of the world's GDP while the latter country's GDP is 10 percent of the world's GDP, the volume of trade between them is proportional to the product of their GDP levels.[85]

A similar calculation can be performed for trade volumes within groups of countries. It yields the prediction that the ratio of the within-group volume of trade relative to the group's joint GDP level is larger the more similar the countries are in size, where a country's size is measured by its GDP relative to the group's joint GDP level. Moreover, this calculation yields a precise measure of country-size similarity (see Helpman, 1987). Figure 4.3 depicts this relationship for 14 industrial countries in

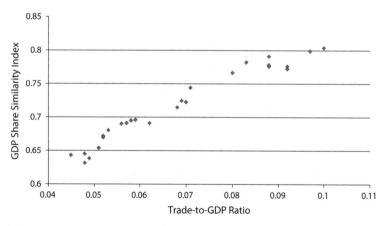

Figure 4.3. Similarity of GDP shares vs. trade-to-GDP ratio: 14 industrial countries, 1956–1981. Data from Helpman (1987).

Helpman's (1987) data, for the years 1956–1981; a point in the figure represents a particular year. The figure shows that in years in which these countries were more similar in size they traded among themselves larger fractions of income. As it happens, they became more similar in size over time and their trade share grew over time.

In less extreme cases, in which some sectors manufacture differentiated products while other sectors produce homogeneous goods, the theory predicts a positive impact of similarity of country size on the ratio of trade volume to GDP, but it also predicts that differences in factor composition raise the trade share. In other words, both size similarity and factor composition differences affect trade volumes.

A more elaborate analysis of the impact of country-size similarity on the volume of bilateral trade flows is provided in Debaere (2005), confirming in a sample of OECD countries that country pairs with more similar GDP levels trade larger fractions of their income. While this relationship holds for the rich countries in his sample, Debaere finds no such relationship in a larger sample that includes both rich and poor countries. This finding is consistent with the view that in a world in which there are sectors with product differentiation and other sectors with homogeneous goods, rich countries trade with each other a disproportionate amount of differentiated products, because they specialize relatively more in differentiated-product industries. Thus differences in factor proportions are less important and intra-industry specialization is more important for trade between rich countries.[86]

In addition to providing a better explanation of trade volumes, product differentiation is central for explaining the data on intra-industry trade. Helpman and Krugman (1985) point out that if all sectors manufacture homogeneous products, then the share of intra-industry trade is zero, and if some sectors manufacture differentiated products, then the share of intra-industry trade is positive. In the data there is large variation in the share of intra-industry trade, as we have seen. To explain it they show that in a simple two-country, two-factor model of international trade in

which there are only two sectors, one supplying homogeneous goods and
the other supplying brands of a differentiated product, the share of intra-
industry trade is smaller the larger the difference in factor composition
across the countries is, holding constant their relative size. In other words,
if goods are produced with capital and labor, the share of intra-industry
trade should be larger the more similar the capital-labor ratios of the two
countries are.

In addition to trade volumes, Helpman (1987) studies empirically the
relationship between the similarity of factor composition and the share
of intra-industry trade. For his sample of 14 OECD countries, he finds
that the share of intra-industry trade is larger in periods in which the
countries' factor endowments are more similar, as measured by similarity
of GDP per capita.[87] This is illustrated in Figure 4.4, in which the horizontal axis measures the share of intra-industry trade within the group
of 14 industrial countries and the vertical axis measures the coefficient
of variation of their GDP per capita, each point for a different year. The

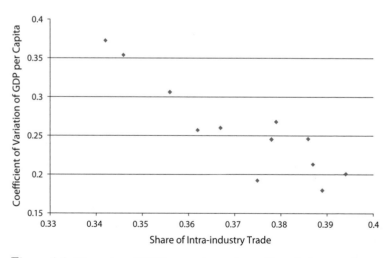

Figure 4.4. Dispersion of GDP per capita vs. share of intra-industry trade:
14 industrial countries, 1970–1981. Data from Helpman (1987).

figure shows a clear negative correlation between dispersion of income per capita and intra-industry trade.

A more detailed analysis of this relationship is provided by Cieślik (2005) for bilateral trade flows in the sample of OECD countries studied by Debaere (2005) and Hummels and Levinsohn (1995). He finds a strong negative correlation between the share of intra-industry trade and the difference between the capital-labor ratios of the two trading countries, when controlling for the sum of the two capital-labor ratios. The need for the latter control is derived from the theoretical model. It follows that while differences in factor composition raise the overall volume of trade, they reduce the share of intra-industry trade.

Monopolistic competition among firms with economies of scale affects trade structure through an additional channel, the so-called home-market effect, which was originally identified by Krugman (1980). The home-market effect leads countries with larger domestic markets for brands of a particular product to specialize in such brands relative to countries with smaller markets. This bias arises in the presence of trade costs, but not without them. The logic is as follows. In the absence of trade costs a firm that manufactures a brand of a differentiated product is indifferent between locating in a small country, such as Belgium, or in a large country, such as the United States, as long as the cost conditions are the same in both countries. The reason is that independently of where the firm manufactures, it can sell to all countries of the world at equal cost. But if trade impediments exist, then the firm prefers to locate in the United States, because it can cheaply supply the larger market and face higher costs in supplying the smaller market only. Yet as more firms locate in the United States, it becomes less attractive for an additional firm to locate there, because competition in the local market becomes fiercer. In the end, more firms have to locate in the larger market than in the smaller one in order for all of them to be equally profitable. What Krugman shows, however, is that the number of firms that locate in the larger market has to be *disproportionately* large; that is, the number of firms divided by market size has to be larger in the larger market. As a result, the larger country exports this industry's products on net.

A number of studies identified home-market effects by examining the impact of variation in demand levels across countries on net trade flows. Davis and Weinstein (1999, 2003) study manufacturing industries in OECD countries and in Japanese regions. In both data sets they estimate a positive impact of local demand on local supply (i.e., a rise in local demand induces an expansion of local supply), with the coefficient exceeding 1 in various differentiated-product sectors. The key finding is a coefficient that exceeds 1, which is consistent with a home-market effect but not with its absence. Head and Ries (2001) report similar findings for trade between Canada and the United States.

Hanson and Xiang (2004) provide the most detailed study of the home-market effect. They classify industries by trade costs and elasticities of substitution, where an elasticity of substitution measures by how much the relative demand for two products rises when their relative cost falls by 1 percent. If, say, their relative demand rises by 5 percent, the elasticity of substitution equals 5, and if their relative demand rises by 2 percent, it equals 2. Sectors with high trade costs and low elasticities of substitution are more prone to home-market effects than sectors with low trade costs and high elasticities of substitution. Intuitively, higher transport costs make the local market more important relative to export markets, while a lower elasticity of substitution across brands makes variety more important in demand.[88] In their industrial classification, pig iron, glassware, tires, and furniture belong to sectors with high freight rates and low elasticities of substitution, while computers, televisions, cameras, and printing machinery belong to sectors with low freight rates and high elasticities of substitution. Using a statistical model that allows them to estimate the differential effect of country size on differences in trade flows across the two types of industries, they find that—indeed— as predicted by the home-market effect, larger countries tend to export relatively more than smaller countries in sectors with high transport costs and low elasticities of substitution.

Although Krugman (1980) focused his analysis on horizontally differentiated products (brands of similar quality with otherwise varying characteristics), the logic of the home-market effect can be extended to vertically differentiated products (brands of different quality).[89] This extension helps in explaining additional features of the data. In particular, unit values of exports differ between rich and poor countries, where the unit value is defined as revenue divided by a quantity measure, such as the number of units exported (e.g., the number of laptops) or the weight of exports (e.g., tons of wheat). Within the same product category, rich countries tend to export goods with higher unit values than those exported by poor countries (see Schott, 2004). This finding is consistent with rich countries exporting goods of higher quality. Since rich countries have relatively more rich people and rich people tend to consume higher-quality products than poor people do, the home-market effect induces rich countries to export higher-quality products. In other words, the home-market effect provides an explanation for why rich countries may have a comparative advantage in high-quality products even when they have no technological advantage in manufacturing these goods.

While the new trade theory rationalizes gravity, intra-industry trade, and home-market effects, it also rationalizes estimates of trade flows that depend on the interaction between sectoral factor intensities and exporting countries' relative factor abundance, which are at the heart of the factor proportions theory. In the previous chapter we discussed the Heckscher-Ohlin factor proportions theory and the empirical work that builds on its insights. Recall that the empirical work focused on the theory's predictions about the *factor content* of trade flows (i.e., the services of various inputs embodied in imports and exports). The main reason for the shift in the empirical work from the theory's predictions about trade in goods to trade in factor content was that in a world with factor price equalization, in which there are few inputs and many products, the theory does not yield clear-cut results concerning sectoral trade flows. Nevertheless, the theory yields very sharp predictions about the factor content of trade flows, predictions that were originally developed by Vanek (1968). The reason for the weak predictions about trade in goods is that with few inputs and many outputs a country's factor endowments do not determine uniquely its sectoral output mix; given the employed ratios of inputs per unit output, there are many ways in which sectoral output levels can be configured to secure full employment of the country's resources. By implication, when output levels are not determined in a unique way, exports and imports are also not determined in a unique way, because net imports are equal to the difference between consumption (absorption) and local production.

This theoretical ambiguity notwithstanding, empirical studies of sectoral trade flows found systematic correlations between net exports and factor intensities. For example, Baldwin (1971) found that in 1962 sectoral U.S. net exports were positively correlated with sectoral skilled-labor intensity and negatively correlated with sectoral capital intensity. Although these types of correlations do not constitute a test of the factor proportions theory, because they do not build on the three-way relationship between country-level factor endowments, industry-level factor intensities, and trade flows (see Leamer and Levinsohn, 1995), they exhibit interesting relationships that are consistent with the theory. In an important contribution, Romalis (2004) shows how to reconcile these conflicting elements by integrating product differentiation into a factor proportions model that admits differences in factor prices across countries, of the type studied by Dornbusch, Fischer, and Samuelson (1980). Romalis uses the model to develop an equation that links a country's sectoral exports to the industry's factor intensity interacted with the country's abundance of the input. A country is expected to export more in an industry that is intensive in inputs with which the country is relatively well endowed. Because of product differentiation, the country also imports products in the same industry, and its imports consist of exports of the country's trade partners, with these exports being governed by similar relationships. He then estimates these relationships with U.S. imports of more than 16,000 commodities from 200 trade partners, using 1998 data aggregated into several hundred industries, and finds strong support for the theoretical predictions.

Figure 4.5 illustrates the relationship between an industry's skilled-labor intensity and the share of the exporting country in U.S. imports, for Germany and Bangladesh.[90] It shows that while Germany's share is higher the more skill-intensive the industry is, Bangladesh's share declines with the sector's skill intensity. This is exactly what the theory predicts,

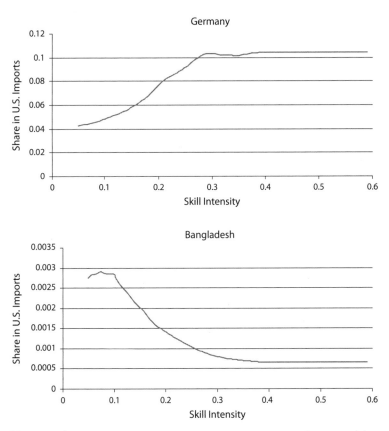

Figure 4.5. Skill intensity and share in U.S. imports in 1998: Germany and Bangladesh. Data from Romalis (2004, figure 1).

because Germany has a relatively large endowment of skilled relative to unskilled workers while Bangladesh has a small endowment of skilled relative to unskilled workers.

Romalis's methodology has been applied by Nunn (2007) to study the impact of law-enforcement institutions on comparative advantage and trade flows.[91] Nunn's point of departure is the observation that the degree of specificity of intermediate inputs varies across industries; in some sectors a large fraction of inputs is product specific, in other sectors only a small fraction of inputs is product specific. If one could write complete contracts, specifying in great detail all the characteristics that an input has to have, and these contracts could be implemented with certainty, then the specificity of inputs would cause no difficulties in the organization of production. A firm would still need to decide whether to produce an input in-house or outsource it, based on various cost considerations discussed in Chapter 6; yet in either case there would exist no distortions of incentives due to specificity considerations. In many instances this is not the case, however; it can be very hard, or impossible, to write a complete contract and implement it in the court of law. As a result, in these cases contracts are incomplete.[92]

When contracts are incomplete, countries with bad legal systems suffer from a cost disadvantage in sectors in which contracting is important, such as sectors with large fractions of product-specific inputs. Consequently, differences across countries in the quality of contract-enforcement institutions affect their relative costs across industries. As a result of these biases in relative costs, countries with better contract-enforcement institutions are expected to export relatively more in sectors with relatively larger fractions of contract-dependent inputs. Naturally, other determinants of comparative advantage, such as those studied by Romalis (2004), are still in force, but the quality of legal systems adds an additional source of variation in relative costs.

Nunn (2007) develops indexes of the importance of contract-dependent inputs for a large number of industries. Using these indexes, he then estimates Romalis-style equations of relative bilateral exports in every industry for a large sample of countries. A ratio of exports depends on differences across the two countries in both endowments and quality of legal institutions, each one interacted with the relevant measure of sectoral intensity. In particular, differences in the relative availability of human capital are interacted with sectoral human capital intensity, and differences in the quality of legal systems are interacted with sectoral measures of contract intensity. According to his estimates, poultry processing, rice milling, and coffee and tea manufacturing belong to the least contract-intensive industries, while air and gas compressor manufacturing, aircraft manufacturing, and electronic computer manufacturing belong to the most contract-intensive industries. A main finding of this research is that, indeed, as predicted by theory, countries with better contract-enforcement institutions export relatively more in contract-intensive sectors. And moreover, these effects are very sizable, larger in magnitude than the impact of capital and labor endowments combined.[93]

4.3 Additional Sources of Gains from Trade

In the previous chapter we discussed gains from trade and distributional conflicts in countries with competitive markets and constant-returns-to-scale technologies. The main argument was that these types of countries gain from trade in the sense that trade raises everybody's welfare when individuals are all alike, and that if individuals are not all alike then the gainers can compensate the losers in a way that makes everyone better off. The key mechanism that drives this result operates through prices: on average, trade leads to an expansion of sectors whose prices are higher in the trade regime and to a contraction of sectors whose prices are lower in the trade regime. As a result, the country can afford to acquire its autarky consumption basket when it trades with other countries, and thereby attains higher welfare.

In the presence of external scale economies, relative price movements that emanate from trade can be similarly beneficial, except that in this case shifts in sectoral output levels impact productivity, as we have seen in section 4.1. Under the circumstances trade is beneficial if it does not lead to a decline in the economy's total factor productivity, or if TFP declines, it does not decline too much. A sufficient condition for gains from trade is therefore that in this economy increasing-returns-to-scale sectors expand on average, or do not contract too much (see Helpman and Krugman, 1985, pp. 64–66). But, as originally pointed out by Graham (1923), this outcome cannot be guaranteed for every country, because trade can push some countries to specialize in traditional sectors with no economies of scale. Nevertheless, this negative effect can be offset to some extent by the fact that in an integrated world, in which countries trade with each other, the concentration of production raises productivity and reduces the costs of manufacturing with increasing-returns technologies, because in a trading world there are many more sales than in a single country. As a result, even if an increasing-returns industry is located in a foreign country, its goods can be acquired via imports at low prices, potentially much lower than the country's consumers pay in autarky. In other words, although in this type of world one cannot be sure that every country gains from trade, there do exist forces that make gains likely, and they are potentially larger than in a world with no economies of scale.

Similar arguments apply in the presence of product differentiation and firm-level economies of scale, of the type discussed in the previous section, except that in this case the relevant measure of output for productivity changes is not at the sectoral level but rather at the firm level. That is, improvements in total factor productivity require an expansion of output per firm rather then per sector. In addition, there are welfare effects from changes in available variety, because a wider variety choice is beneficial independently of productivity outcomes. For these reasons, the aggregate impact of trade on welfare includes the traditional effect of relative prices, the effect of productivity, and the effect of variety (see

Helpman and Krugman, 1985, chapter 9). Again, one cannot guarantee gains from trade for all countries, and especially not if countries greatly differ from each other, but there are strong forces pushing toward such gains. First, because every firm serves the entire world economy, it is most likely that the output of a representative firm in an industry is higher in a trade regime than in autarky, in which case trade raises TFP. Second, because in every sector variety is available from all producers around the globe, it is most likely that more variety is available in the trade regime than in autarky. And even if one of these positive channels of influence does not work (e.g., output per firm declines in some industries), this shortfall can be more than compensated for by other sources of gains from trade.

The presence of multiple channels of gains from trade can mute conflicts of interest among different sources of income, such as ownership of different factors of production. We have seen in the previous chapter that in a competitive world with constant-returns-to-scale technologies, the distributional conflicts are unavoidable; in the absence of compensation mechanisms, some factors of production necessarily gain from trade while others lose. This need not be the case in the presence of product differentiation and firm-specific economies of scale, as pointed out by Krugman (1981). In particular, growth in variety can compensate factor owners for declines in relative income. As an example, consider a world in which goods are produced with labor and capital. Then, in the absence of product differentiation and scale economies, the opening of trade raises the real income of a country's relatively abundant factor of production and reduces the real income of a country's relatively scarce factor of production. Under the circumstances, a country that is relatively rich in capital sees an increase in the real income of capital owners when it integrates into the world economy. But if there is product differentiation and trade leads to an expansion of variety, then workers may gain from trade too, although proportionately less than capital owners. Such gains are ensured when countries do not differ from one another too much in relative factor endowments, but not if they have very different quantities of capital per worker.

Models of monopolistic competition help bridge the gap between theory and evidence concerning broad patterns of international trade within and across industries. These patterns and the underlying theory were reviewed in this chapter. The next chapter examines in more detail trade structure within industries and the international organization of production.

5

Across Firms within Industries

The integration of economies of scale and monopolistic competition into traditional trade theory was a major intellectual achievement that provided a framework for better understanding the structure of world trade. As we saw in the previous chapter, this approach emphasizes the importance of the range of products available in a country, it suggests new sources of comparative advantage, and its empirical predictions find support in the data.

Despite the desirable features of these trade models from the 1980s, they proved inadequate to explain a range of empirical findings that emerged in the 1990s from new firm-level data sets. These findings are related to a key property of industrial structure—namely, that within a typical sector, firms vary greatly in size, productivity, composition of inputs, wages, and participation in foreign trade. Moreover, firms that trade are systematically different from those that do not trade, and multinational corporations—which own production plants or distribution outlets in multiple countries—are systematically different too. In combination with changing trends in the patterns of foreign trade and foreign direct investment, these findings triggered another rethinking of trade theory.

5.1 Exporting vs. Nonexporting Firms

In the 1990s a number of studies examined the characteristics of firms within industries to assess the extent to which they differ by trade status. Bernard and Jensen (1995, 1999) were the first to address this issue with data for the United States; their work was followed by studies of other countries, including Canada, Colombia, France, Mexico, Morocco, Spain, and Taiwan.[94] These studies found that only a small fraction of firms export, that exporting firms are larger and more productive than nonexporters, and that export status tends to persist. The last attribute was interpreted to manifest the large sunk costs of exporting (i.e., that a firm that wishes to penetrate a foreign market has to bear substantial market-specific setup costs to sell in that market).[95] Das, Roberts, and Tybout (2007) estimate such costs to be over $400,000 for Colombian small producers and somewhat lower for large producers.

Table 5.1 presents data on exporting firms in the manufacturing sector. It shows that in the United States only 18 percent of manufacturing firms export, and similarly in France, Japan, Chile, and Colombia. This fraction is substantially larger in Norway, however, where nearly 40 percent of the firms export. In addition, industries vary widely by fraction of exporters; in some sectors this fraction is larger than the average reported in Table 5.1, while in other sectors it is much smaller. In the United States,

Table 5.1. Share of Manufacturing Firms that Export, in Percent

Country	Year	Exporting Firms (%)
U.S.A.	2002	18.0
Norway	2003	39.2
France	1986	17.4
Japan	2000	20.0
Chile	1999	20.9
Colombia	1990	18.2

Source: World Trade Organization (2008, table 5).

for example, only 5 percent of firms engaged in printing and related support export, and 7 percent engaged in furniture and related products export. On the other side, 33 percent of machinery manufacturing firms export, and 38 percent export in computer and electronic products.[96]

Firms that export are larger and more productive than nonexporting firms by a substantial margin. In the United States exporters employ about twice as many workers as nonexporters, and the value of their total sales is approximately double. In addition, the value-added per worker of exporters is 11 percent larger than the value-added per worker of nonexporters, and the total factor productivity of exporters exceeds the TFP of nonexporters by 3 percent.[97] Also, as can be seen from Table 5.2, exports are highly skewed toward large firms. In the United States the top 1 percent of exporters sell abroad 81 percent of U.S. manufacturing exports, while the top 10 percent sell abroad 96 percent. In Belgium, France, Germany, Norway, and the United Kingdom, the top 1 percent of exporters have lower shares of exports than U.S. firms do, but their shares are still substantial, between 42 percent and 59 percent. And the top 10 percent of exporters in these countries control between 80 percent and 91 percent of exports, very large shares indeed. Finally, exporters sell the majority of their output in the home market and export only a fraction of their total sales. For example, in 2002, exporting firms in U.S.

Table 5.2. Share of Exports of Manufactures-Exporting Firms, by Firm Size, in Percent

Country	Year	Top 1% of firms	Top 10% of firms
U.S.A.	2002	81	96
Belgium	2003	48	84
France	2003	44	84
Germany	2003	59	90
Norway	2003	53	91
U.K.	2003	42	80

Source: World Trade Organization (2008, table 6).

manufacturing delivered an average of 14 percent of their total shipments to foreign countries, with the fraction of these exports varying between 7 percent and 21 percent across industries.[98]

To explain these patterns in the data, Melitz (2003) developed a theoretical model that changed trade theory fundamentally.[99] For expositional purposes I will discuss a simplified version of his framework that brings out the economic intuition behind the main arguments. Consider a sector that produces differentiated products under conditions of monopolistic competition, as described in the previous chapter. Unlike the previous chapter, however, now assume that a firm that enters the industry faces uncertainty regarding its TFP. That is, a firm bears an entry cost that covers the development of its brand and the technology to manufacture it, but it discovers only ex-post—after bearing this cost— whether its productivity is high or low. As a result, firms form expectations about the profitability of entry, and they enter as long as their *expected* profits are high enough to cover their entry cost. Entry proceeds until expected profits just equal the entry cost. Evidently, this condition is in the spirit of Chamberlin's free-entry condition for the large-group case, accounting for the risk of entry.

To form expectations about the profitability of entry, a firm needs to form expectations about its profits at different productivity levels, and for this it needs to form a business strategy for every productivity level. In particular, it has to decide at what productivity levels it is best to forfeit the entry cost and close shop, at what productivity levels it can make money by selling to domestic customers, and at what productivity levels it can make money by exporting.[100] Melitz (2003) assumes that a firm has to bear a fixed cost of manufacturing if it stays in the industry and an additional fixed cost of exporting if it chooses to sell some fraction of its output abroad, as suggested by the empirical evidence. In addition, exporting generates variable trade costs; they may arise from freight and insurance fees, from a destination country's tariffs, or from other barriers to trade. Under these circumstances we can express the profitability of staying in the industry, after the entry cost has been sunk, by means of Figure 5.1.

The upper curve in the figure describes profits from domestic sales (i.e., revenue minus variable production costs minus the fixed cost of production) as a function of a firm's productivity; firms that are more productive are more profitable in the domestic market. A firm with zero productivity cannot manufacture, but it has to bear, nevertheless, the fixed cost of production as long as it stays in the industry. For this reason, at zero productivity, profits are negative at point *d*, below the horizontal axis. The distance between point *d* and the horizontal axis represents the fixed cost of production. As the firm becomes more productive these profits rise, and at point *D* they become zero. Profits continue to rise with productivity, and they are positive for all productivity levels to the right of *D*.

The lower curve in the figure describes profits from export sales. They too are negative for a firm with zero productivity, and the distance between the horizontal axis and point *x* represents the fixed cost of exporting that

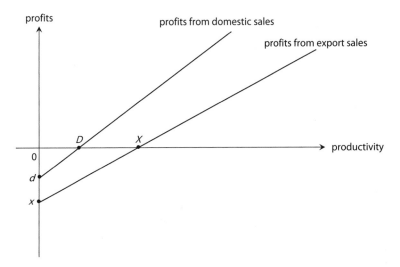

Figure 5.1. Profits of firms with different productivity levels.

a firm has to bear in addition to the fixed cost of production. Profits from export sales rise with productivity, they become zero at point X, and continue to rise further at productivity levels to the right of X. It follows that firms with productivity to the left of X lose money from exporting while firms with productivity to the right of X make money from export sales. The location of these profit curves ensures that X is to the right of D. This is no accident; X to the right of D fits a pattern of industrial structure that is consistent with the evidence.

In Figure 5.1, firms with productivity to the left of D can make money neither from domestic sales nor from exporting; their profits are negative from each of these activities. As a result their best strategy is to exit the industry in order to avoid bearing the fixed cost of manufacturing. This strategy leads to zero profits, albeit only after sacrificing the entry cost. Firms with productivity between points D and X choose a different strategy; they make profits from domestic sales but lose money from export sales. Therefore they maximize profits by serving the domestic market but not the foreign market. That is, they choose to stay in the industry without exporting. Finally, firms with productivity to the right of X make money from domestic sales as well as from exporting. Therefore their business strategy is to serve the domestic market as well as the foreign market. In short, in this sort of industry the least-productive firms choose to exit, intermediate-productivity firms choose to sell only to domestic customers, and the most-productive firms choose to sell to foreign as well as to domestic customers. This sorting pattern is consistent with the evidence that only a fraction of firms export, that exporters sell only a portion of their output to foreign customers, that exporters are larger and more productive than nonexporters (they are larger because higher-productivity firms employ more workers, produce more goods, and thus have higher revenue), and that the distribution of export sales is skewed toward larger firms (because larger firms export more and therefore have higher revenue from export sales). As is clear from this analysis, Melitz offered a simple and compelling explanation of these facts. And although his model does not explain why exporters pay higher wages than nonexporters (in this theoretical framework all firms pay the same wages), we shall see later that a modified version of the model generates this wage prediction as well.

Studies of trade liberalization find repeatedly that much of the reallocation of resources in response to falling trade barriers takes place within industries rather than across them. Balassa (1966, 1967) was the first to note that the formation of the European Common Market, the predecessor of the now much-expanded European Union, did not lead to major reallocations of resources across industries, as would be predicted by traditional trade theory. He made the following astute observation:

> As regards the impact of tariff reductions on resource allocation, the predominance of intraindustry, as against interindustry, specialization in manufactured goods traded among the industrial countries is the relevant consideration. With national product differentiation in consumer goods, machinery, and intermediate goods at higher levels of fabrication, trade liberalization does not entail massive shifts of resources from import-competing to export industries as presumed by the traditional textbook explanation, but leads instead to changes in the product composition of individual industries . . . .
>
> However, tariff reductions will result in interindustry shifts of resources in the case of standardized products where international exchange is determined largely by intercountry differences in relative costs. (Balassa 1967, p. 93)

And even more pointedly, recent studies of trade liberalization, which use detailed firm-level data, such as Tybout and Westbrook (1995) for Mexico, Pavcnik (2002) for Chile, and Trefler (2004) for Canada, find large market share reallocations within industries from low- to high-productivity enterprises, as well as the exit of low-productivity firms. Can these shifts within industries be explained by the model? The answer is yes.

Consider a reduction in trade barriers. This lowers the variable costs of exporting. As a result, profits from export sales rise, and the lower curve in Figure 5.1 shifts upward. This rise in the profitability of exporting firms is accompanied by an expansion of their output and export sales, which leads to a shift in market share from domestic firms that do not export to exporters. Since the expansion of exporting firms raises demand for domestic factors of production and, in the case of a multilateral trade liberalization, also exposes the domestic market to more foreign competition, input costs rise in the domestic market and demand per product falls. These changes cut into the profits of all firms, but do not fully offset the rise in profits of exporters. The decline in profits of domestic firms reduces the upper curve in the figure, implying that some of the low-productivity firms, whose productivity is to the right of point D but close to it—that is, which were marginally profitable before—lose money in the new circumstances. These firms therefore close shop and exit the industry. Evidently, trade liberalization leads to the exit of the least-productive firms and market share reallocation from low-productivity domestic firms to high-productivity exporters, which taken together raise the industry's average productivity. This is an important observation, because it suggests that powerful economic forces are at work reconfiguring industrial structures in a way that raises sectoral productivity levels.

Are these effects sizable? The Canada-U.S. Free Trade Agreement (FTA) of 1989, which has been studied extensively by many scholars, provides a good illustration. According to Trefler (2004), in 1988 the average Canadian tariff on imports from the United States was 8.1 percent. Moreover, tariffs in excess of 10 percent applied to a quarter of Canadian industries. On the U.S. side, tariffs were much lower, averaging only 4 percent. Trefler had access to plant-level data, which enabled him to study the impact of the FTA on labor productivity in great detail. He found that the FTA raised labor productivity in Canadian manufacturing by 7.4 percent, which is a very large percentage indeed, and that the productivity gains in the most impacted import-competing industries were about twice as high. Because there was little gain in productivity at the plant level, most of these gains are attributed to market share reallocations in favor of high-productivity plants and the exit of low-productivity plants. In other words, the Canadian experience conforms to the theoretical analysis.

Reallocations within sectors can be studied in conjunction with traditional forces of comparative advantage. Bernard, Redding, and Schott (2007) analyze a model of monopolistic competition with two inputs, two sectors, and two countries, in which within every industry there are heterogeneous firms and fixed and variable trade costs. To ease the analysis, they assume that factor proportions are similar across activities within a sector, but that they differ across sectors.[101] Under these circumstances, trade raises total factor productivity in every sector in every country. Moreover, the rise in TFP is driven by the exit of the least-productive firms and share reallocations from less- to more-productive firms. Interestingly, the rise in productivity is not the same in all sectors, and it exhibits a different bias in each of the countries. In particular, TFP rises proportionately more in each country's comparatively advantaged sector; that is, the sector that is intensive in the input with which the country is relatively well endowed. By implication, the larger gain in productivity takes place in different sectors in different countries. Moreover, this result implies that every country exports on net in a sector with a relatively higher productivity gain, so it may appear that trade is driven by Ricardian forces of comparative advantage. Yet in this case the Ricardian productivity advantage is generated by Heckscher-Ohlin forces of comparative advantage, meaning that the country that is relatively well endowed with a particular input happens to also have relatively higher TFP in the industry that uses this input intensively. It follows that in this world, factor proportions–type comparative advantage is inseparable from relative productivity–type comparative advantage.

5.2 Quantitative Assessment

We have seen in Chapter 4 that explicit recognition of the response of variety choice to trade helps explain various empirical phenomena and enriches our understanding of economic adjustments to trade liberalization. It still remains an open question whether these adjustments are quantitatively important. Because only a few studies have measured explicitly the adjustments due to the extensive margin of trade (the part of trade that results from changes in the number of varieties of traded products), the evaluation of these effects is only tentative.

As we discussed in the previous chapter, the gravity equation is the main tool for empirical investigation of international trade flows; it is used to estimate the impact on trade of variables such as distance, currency areas, and free trade agreements. When applied to large samples of countries, this approach cannot use firm-level data (which cannot be pooled together from individual countries because of confidentiality restrictions) and has to rely instead on country-industry-level data sets. Under these circumstances, scholars focused in the past on refining their estimation techniques to improve the accuracy of the estimates, but paid little attention to the separation of the extensive from the intensive margin of trade.[102] Helpman, Melitz, and Rubinstein (2008) show, however, that it is possible to estimate separately the intensive and extensive margins of trade from aggregate data by utilizing parts of the data that typically had not been used before, namely, observations of zero trade flows. For this purpose they develop a multicountry generalized version of Melitz's (2003) model, which admits differences in fixed and variable trade costs across distinct country pairs, and they develop a two-stage estimation procedure for the parameters of this model.

The main idea behind Helpman, Melitz, and Rubinstein's approach is that a firm's volume of exports to a given country does not depend on its fixed export cost. However, the decision to export does depend on this fixed cost. For this reason the lack of exports from, say, Germany to Gabon implies that even the most-productive German firm cannot cover the fixed export cost to Gabon with the revenue from sales in Gabon net of variable costs of production and exporting. Considering all possible bilateral export flows between pairs of countries, one can therefore use the distinction between the flows that are positive and those that are zero to estimate an equation that provides information about the productivity cutoffs that make exports profitable.[103] These productivity cutoffs in turn provide information about the fraction of firms that find it profitable to export.

It is then possible to use this first-stage equation to forecast the fraction of exporters, and use this projection in a second-stage equation of the standard gravity type to estimate separately the impact of various trade impediments or enhancers on the intensive and extensive margins of trade. Helpman, Melitz, and Rubinstein find that the impact of distance between country pairs (a trade impediment) on the intensive margin of trade is about two-thirds of what is normally estimated, which represents a substantial bias, and they find a similar bias in the estimated impact of a currency union (a trade enhancer). Importantly, the biases vary substantially across countries with different characteristics, such as levels of development, because the impact of the extensive margin of trade varies considerably across country pairs. For example, the overall impact of distance on trade flows tends to be smallest across country pairs with high income per capita, and largest across country pairs with low income per capita. This impact is intermediate for pairs of countries in which one country has high income per capita while the other has low income per capita. More specifically, the largest effect of distance on exports is roughly three times as large as the smallest effect. In other words, not only do standard estimates overstate the role of the intensive margin of trade, they also miss an important source of heterogeneity in the sensitivity of trade to impediments and enhancers, which is driven by the extensive margin of trade.

Balistreri, Hillberry, and Rutherford (2008) estimate an elaborate model of international trade, which divides the world into nine regions and seven sectors. The regions are described in Table 5.3. The sectors include agriculture, manufacturing, energy, and services, but only manufacturing is modeled as a sector with monopolistic competition and heterogeneous firms. Other than its inclusion of firm heterogeneity and monopolistic competition in the manufacturing sector, this model is a

Table 5.3. Welfare Gains from Halving Tariffs on Manufactures, in Percent

Region	Without firm heterogeneity	With firm heterogeneity
China	0.3	1.3
North America	−0.0	0.0
Latin America	0.1	0.5
Europe	0.1	0.2
Eastern Europe and former Soviet Union	−0.1	−0.3
Japan plus Korea and Taiwan	0.1	0.3
Rest of Asia	0.3	1.1
Australia and New Zealand	0.4	1.4
Rest of the World	−0.2	−0.7

Source: Balistreri, Hillberry, and Rutherford (2008, table 8).

"standard" model commonly used for trade policy analysis, which assumes competitive markets. As a result, Balistreri, Hillberry, and Rutherford can compare the impact of trade policies in two alternative setups: one without firm heterogeneity in manufactures (a standard formulation) and one with firm heterogeneity.[104] Differences in outcomes can then be attributed to firm heterogeneity and the extensive margin of trade.

Table 5.3 reports the aggregate (summed over all people) welfare gains from a 50 percent reduction in manufacturing tariffs. Changes in the prices of exported relative to imported products (i.e., the terms of trade) are an important source of a country's welfare gains or losses, especially in the absence of firm heterogeneity. When the relative prices of exportables rise, a country gains, and when they fall, a country loses. With firm heterogeneity there are additional welfare effects from changes in the average productivity of firms in the manufacturing industry and the number of available brands.

To gauge the size of these welfare changes, it is important to bear in mind that, in the data, manufactures account for only 25 percent of aggregate output, that only about 15 percent of manufactures are traded across the regions, and that the average tariff on manufactures is

9.3 percent. Therefore, in the exercise reported in the table, the tariff cuts are small, less than 5 percent on average, and they apply to a quarter of output. Under the circumstances the welfare effects reported in Table 5.3 are substantial. To begin with, most regions gain from trade liberalization, although some lose: in the traditional setup, Eastern Europe loses a tenth of 1 percent and the Rest of the World loses two-tenths of 1 percent. In the setup with heterogeneous firms, these regions lose even more: Eastern Europe loses three-tenths of 1 percent while the Rest of the World loses seven-tenths of 1 percent. Nevertheless, the simple average gain is about four times as high in the presence of firm heterogeneity: 0.422 of a percent compared to 0.111. The difference in gains is particularly pronounced for China, Latin America, the Rest of Asia, and Australia and New Zealand. For China the gains are four times as large in the presence of heterogeneity and monopolistic competition, for Latin America they are five times as high, for the Rest of Asia they are almost four times as high, and for Australia and New Zealand they are more than three times as high.

While product differentiation and firm heterogeneity introduce new channels of gains from trade and trade liberalization, the extent of these gains is highly uncertain.[105] By some measures the penetration of foreign supplies into the domestic market impacts domestic entry in a way that fully offsets potential welfare changes, making the gains depend on the exposure to trade overall but not on the degree of product differentiation. Arkolakis, Demidova, Klenow, and Rodríguez-Clare (2008) show this result analytically for one-sector economies, and they estimate small gains from trade liberalization in Costa Rica.[106] The one-sector structure of their model is very restrictive, however. For example, the Balistreri, Hillberry, and Rutherford (2008) model has multiple sectors. As a result, trade liberalization in their manufacturing sector leads to expansion of employment in this industry, which cannot happen in the one-sector world of Arkolakis, Demidova, Klenow, and Rodríguez-Clare. This contributes in turn to the large product differentiation–related gains from trade liberalization that show up in their own simulations. As of now, the debate about these issues has not been resolved.

5.3 Unemployment and Inequality

I have discussed in this and previous chapters a number of mechanisms through which international trade impacts labor markets, benefitting or harming workers. In particular, we have seen that international trade benefits workers if the country's exports are labor-intensive but not if the country's imports are labor-intensive. And we have seen that this type of distributional conflict between labor and other factors of production is muted when product differentiation contributes to gains from trade. Finally, we have seen that if in addition to product differentiation there is firm heterogeneity, international trade raises TFP in both import-competing and exporting industries (with a disproportional impact on the comparatively advantaged sectors), thereby introducing an additional channel for gains in real wages.

Those discussions focused on economies with full employment. Yet in many instances changes in world markets exert pressures that lead to changes in a country's employment opportunities and in its rate of unemployment. Such changes can be temporary, confined to a transition period during which an economy adjusts to new external conditions, or they can be more lasting as a result of long-run structural changes. While temporary spurts of unemployment are a major policy concern, so are structural features of labor markets. To illustrate, in October 1997 the European Union amended its agreement by the Treaty of Amsterdam, which included a title on employment, making employment policies a priority. A month later, in November 1997, the extraordinary European Council meeting in Luxembourg launched the European Employment Strategy, "developed in order to encourage exchange of information and joint discussions by all Member States, thus trying to find solutions or best practices together which could help creating [*sic*] more and better jobs in every Member State."[107] Two and a half years later, during the European Council meeting in Lisbon in March 2000, the heads of state launched the Lisbon Agenda, designed for the European Union "to become the most competitive and dynamic knowledge-based economy in the world capable of sustainable economic growth with more and better jobs and greater social cohesion . . . . This strategy is designed to enable the Union to regain the conditions for full employment, and to strengthen regional cohesion in the European Union."[108] What exactly should the European Union do to achieve these objectives? The United Kingdom, for example, has been particularly concerned with lack of labor market flexibility in countries such as France, Italy, and Spain, and it has been promoting labor market reforms. To assess these types of policies it is necessary to introduce labor market frictions into the analysis.

Frictions in labor markets come in many forms. In some cases wages do not decline when the demand for labor slackens. This may result from the power of labor unions to prevent downward wage flexibility, or from a notion of "fair wages" ingrained in the workers' perception. In other cases the information about available jobs or qualified workers is highly imperfect, leading to the coexistence of unemployed workers on the one hand and unfulfilled job vacancies on the other. With imperfect information workers may wait for better job opportunities and firms may wait for better-qualified job applicants. Hiring is costly to firms, and so is firing. Firing costs often arise from administrative procedures and severance pay imposed by governments or labor unions. In short, there are multiple reasons for labor market frictions.

Labor market rigidities vary substantially across countries, as shown in Table 5.4 for three measures of friction: difficulty of hiring, rigidity of hours, and difficulty of redundancy. In the table the countries are ordered by the average index of these rigidities.[109] According to these data, the United States and Uganda have the most flexible labor markets while Spain and Morocco have the most rigid. Evidently, labor market frictions are low in some low-income and some high-income countries, and

Table 5.4.   Indexes of Labor Market Frictions, from 0–100

Country	Difficulty of Hiring	Rigidity of Hours	Difficulty of Redundancy
United States	0	0	0
Uganda	0	0	0
Rwanda	11	0	10
United Kingdom	11	20	0
Japan	11	7	30
OECD	**27**	**30**	**23**
Italy	33	40	40
Mexico	33	20	70
Russia	33	40	40
Germany	33	53	40
France	67	60	30
Spain	78	40	30
Morocco	89	40	50

Source: Botero et al. (2004). The numbers reported in this table are indexes, with a higher index representing more rigidity. They were downloaded from the World Bank's website, http://www.doingbusiness.org/ExploreTopics/EmployingWorkers/ on September 25, 2009.

they also are high in some low-income and some high-income countries. Among members of the European Union, the United Kingdom has low labor market frictions (significantly below the OECD average) while Germany, Italy, and Spain have high frictions (significantly above the OECD average).

Empirical research suggests that differences in labor market frictions are important determinants of unemployment. Blanchard and Wolfers (2000), for example, show that the response of European countries to changing economic conditions varies in ways that depend on their labor market characteristics. And Nickell, Nunziata, Ochel, and Quintini (2002) show that changes over time in labor market characteristics are important determinants of the evolution of unemployment in OECD countries. These findings suggest that trade liberalization may impact countries differently, depending on their labor market conditions. Moreover, changes in labor market conditions in one country can affect its trade partners, and the ways in which a trade partner is affected may depend on frictions in its own labor market. In other words, labor market frictions impact interdependence across trading countries. In this section I explore how some of these frictions work.

Although a large literature on trade and labor market frictions exists, I focus on search and matching (the difficulty of workers finding jobs and firms filling vacancies), as developed in Diamond (1982a,b) and Mortensen and Pissarides (1994).[110] This approach has proved very useful for explaining structural unemployment, and search and matching has been shown to influence comparative advantage.[111] Because this approach was designed to deal with structural unemployment, its principal focus is on long-term outcomes rather than on short-run fluctuations or temporary periods of adjustment to changing economic conditions.[112]

The search-and-matching approach to labor markets envisions a situation in which firms post vacancies and workers search for employment. Frictions in the labor market prevent all vacancies from being filled and all workers from finding jobs. Instead, the fraction of vacancies that are filled and the fraction of workers who find jobs are determined by a *matching function* that summarizes the conditions in the market place, where the aggregate number of matches depends on the aggregate number of vacancies and the aggregate number of workers searching for jobs. In July 2009 there were 2.4 million job openings in the United States and 15.2 million unemployed workers.[113] That is, there were unfilled vacancies on the one hand and workers searching for jobs on the other. Although the number of unemployed was large in the summer of 2009 because of the recession, the coexistence of both unfilled vacancies and unemployed workers is a permanent feature of the economic landscape.[114]

Helpman and Itskhoki (2010) examine ways in which labor market frictions impact interdependence across countries. They present an analytical framework that can address questions such as "What are the impacts of a country's labor market frictions on its trade partners? How does the removal of trade impediments affect countries with different labor market frictions?" For this purpose they develop a model with two economies that produce both homogeneous products and differentiated products, and in which search and matching take place in each sector. Workers search for jobs in the sector with the highest expected income. Because workers are identical, this implies that expected income from searching for a job is the same in each of the sectors. Firms enter every industry and post vacancies. The number of vacancies posted by firms and the number of workers searching for jobs determine (via the matching function) the number of hires. The probability that a vacancy is filled equals the ratio of aggregate hires in the industry to aggregate vacancies. Similarly, the probability that a worker finds employment equals the ratio of aggregate hires in the industry to the number of workers searching for employment. The latter probability provides a measure of labor market tightness; the higher the probability of employment the tighter the labor market is. The degree of labor market tightness may differ in the two industries. Such differences can result from differing costs of posting vacancies or from differing efficiency levels of the matching process,[115] and they lead to differences in hiring costs and unemployment rates across sectors.[116]

Differences in sectoral rates of unemployment are an important empirical phenomenon. According to the Bureau of Labor Statistics, in 2008 the U.S. rates of unemployment were 3.1 percent in mining, 10.6 percent in construction, 5.8 percent in manufacturing, 5.9 percent in wholesale and retail trade, 5.1 percent in transportation and utilities, 3.9 percent in financial activities, 6.5 percent in professional and business services, 3.5 percent in education and health services, 8.6 percent in leisure and hospitality, 5.3 percent in other services, and 9.2 percent in agricultural and related private wage and salary work.[117] When sectoral rates of unemployment differ, changes in search patterns for jobs across sectors impact the aggregate rate of unemployment.

After the matching process, every firm bargains with its workers over wages.[118] Because both the hiring process and finding employment are costly, both the firm and its workers have bargaining power. This leads to a wage rate that equals the hiring cost of a worker. Therefore, due to the fact that the hiring cost is the same for every firm in a given industry, every firm in such an industry pays the same wage rate. This implies that high- as well as low-productivity firms in the differentiated sector pay the same wage rates.

As in Melitz (2003) (discussed in section 5.1), a firm pays an entry cost, after which it discovers how productive it is. Then it can choose to exit, stay and serve only the domestic market, or stay and serve both the domestic and foreign markets. Depending on its productivity and its desired business strategy, a firm chooses to post vacancies in order to hire workers. In this context the result that wages equal the hiring cost means that all firms—independently of how productive they are and whether they choose to serve only the domestic market or also to export—end up paying the same wage rate. Under these circumstances, a worker is indifferent between being matched with a high- or a low-productivity firm, and similarly an exporting or a nonexporting firm. Moreover, there is a productivity cutoff below which firms find it most profitable to exit and a higher productivity cutoff above which firms find it profitable to export. In between these cutoffs, firms find it profitable to stay in the industry but serve only the domestic market, as depicted in Figure 5.1.

In this setup both countries have the same cost of hiring in the homogeneous-product sector, yet they may have different hiring costs in the differentiated-product sector, depending on the relative levels of labor market frictions in the two sectors. Assuming that the countries are identical, except possibly in terms of labor market frictions, then implies that the country with the higher cost of hiring in the differentiated-product sector imports differentiated products on net and exports homogeneous goods. A lower cost of hiring in the differentiated sector leads to comparative advantage in differentiated products.

A reduction of the variable trade cost raises TFP in the differentiated-product sectors of both countries, similar to Melitz (2003). Yet a country that manages to reduce labor market frictions in its differentiated-product sector raises its own TFP in this sector, but reduces TFP in the trade partner's differentiated-product sector. Intuitively, lower labor market frictions in the differentiated-product sector reduce the cost of hiring, making the sector more competitive in world markets. By implication, they make this same sector less competitive in the trade partner country. Consequently, shifts in competitiveness translate into shifts in productivity.

The last result illustrates an important channel of interdependence across countries through labor market frictions: labor market conditions in one country affect the economic performance of its trade partner. In the context of the European Union's employment strategy, it suggests that labor market reforms in a country such as France may hurt other countries, such as Spain or the United Kingdom, even if these reforms improve French productivity.

The effects of a lowering of labor market frictions in one country are not confined to productivity; they also impact welfare levels. In this economic environment, welfare rises in the reforming country and declines in its trade partner. This contrasts with reductions in variable trade costs in the differentiated sector, which benefit every country.[119] Nevertheless, coordinated reductions—at a common rate—of labor market frictions in the differentiated-product sectors of both countries benefit both of them.

Labor market rigidities play a central role in shaping unemployment. We have already noted that the rate of unemployment in a particular industry is influenced by the tightness of its labor market, which depends in turn on the sector's labor market frictions. A sector's unemployment is higher the more rigid its labor market is. The economy-wide rate of unemployment equals the weighted average of the sectoral rates of unemployment, with the fraction of workers searching for jobs in an industry serving as the industry's weight. As a result, an economy's rate of unemployment can change either because its sectoral rates of unemployment change or because the distribution of workers across industries changes.

The latter depends in turn on the employment opportunities available to workers in different industries.

An implication of this reasoning is that trade reforms that do not influence sectoral rates of unemployment can change the economy-wide rate of unemployment only if they lead to shifts in the relative attractiveness of the two sectors for workers searching for jobs. In particular, a trade reform that reduces variable trade costs in the differentiated-product sector attracts more workers into this industry. As a result, in trading countries with similar labor market frictions, each country's aggregate unemployment rate rises if and only if the differentiated-product sector's labor market is less tight than the homogeneous-product sector's labor market.

The determinants of unemployment are richer in economies with large asymmetries. Figures 5.2 and 5.3 illustrate changes in countrywide rates of unemployment of two trading countries in response to changes in variable trade costs and to changes in labor market frictions in one of

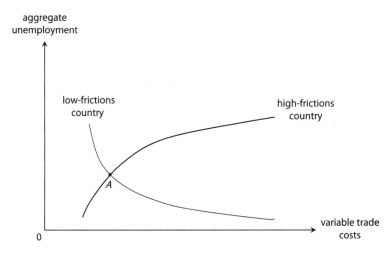

Figure 5.2. Changes in a country's aggregate unemployment in response to rising variable trade costs.

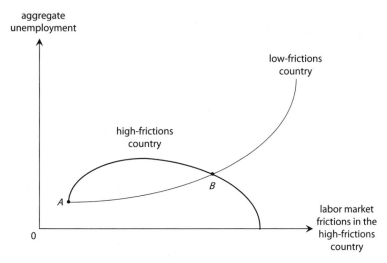

Figure 5.3. Changes in a country's aggregate unemployment in response to rising labor market frictions in the differentiated sector of the high-frictions country.

the countries.[120] In both figures the thick curve depicts changes in the country with higher labor market frictions in the differentiated-product sector, say France, while the thin curve depicts changes in the country with relatively lower labor market frictions in the differentiated sector, say the United Kingdom. Figure 5.2 illustrates a case in which the rate of unemployment rises with variable trade costs in France and declines in the United Kingdom. Moreover, it shows that the high-frictions country has higher unemployment than its trade partner when variable trade costs are high (to the right of point A) and lower unemployment than its trade partner when variable trade costs are low (to the left of A). Evidently, a higher rate of unemployment does not necessarily reflect higher labor market frictions.

In Figure 5.3 the horizontal axis measures labor market frictions in the differentiated-product sector of the country in which these frictions are higher. At point A both countries have the same frictions in both sectors, while to the right of *A* frictions rise in the differentiated-product sector of one country, which becomes the high-frictions country, and do not change in its trade partner. Evidently, at *A*, where both countries have the same frictions, they also have the same aggregate rate of unemployment. As the frictions rise in the high-frictions country, France, its rate of unemployment rises initially and declines eventually; that is, it has a humped shape. In the United Kingdom the rate of unemployment rises continuously. Moreover, France has a higher rate of unemployment than the United Kingdom as long as the differences in their labor market frictions are not too large (they are to the left of point *B*). For large differences, however (to the right of *B*), France has a lower rate of unemployment. We see that the rate of unemployment does not reflect a country's labor market frictions; the rate of unemployment can be higher or lower in the high-frictions country.

The humped shape of the unemployment rate in France stems from the fact that, by assumption, France has a higher rate of sectoral unemployment in the differentiated sector than in the homogeneous sector. As a result, raising labor market frictions in France's differentiated sector raises the sector's rate of unemployment, but it also reduces the number of French workers searching for jobs in this industry. The former effect raises the economy-wide rate of unemployment while the latter effect reduces it. On balance the former effect dominates initially while the latter effect dominates eventually, leading to the humped shape. In the United Kingdom the rate of unemployment is rising because this country's sectoral rates of unemployment do not change, but the rising labor market frictions in France make the differentiated sector in the United Kingdom more competitive, as a result of which more workers search for jobs in the United Kingdom's differentiated sector. Because, by assumption, in the United Kingdom the sectoral rate of unemployment is higher in the differentiated sector than in the homogeneous sector, this labor reallocation raises the United Kingdom's economy-wide rate of unemployment.

A number of conclusions emerge from this discussion. First, while trade or trade liberalization may negatively impact a country's rate of unemployment, the rise in unemployment does not reflect welfare losses; that is, a country's aggregate welfare can rise despite the rise in its unemployment. Second, in a cross-country comparison, unemployment rates are not necessarily negatively correlated with welfare; a country with higher unemployment can have higher welfare. This observation is related to a third: cross-country differences in rates of unemployment are not necessarily positively correlated with differences in labor market frictions; it is possible for a country with higher labor market frictions to have lower unemployment. This comes out clearly in the comparison of the United States and Portugal in Blanchard and Portugal (2001); while labor market frictions were systematically lower in the United States than in Portugal, the latter had higher rates of unemployment than the United States in some periods and lower rates of unemployment in other periods. Fourth, while reductions in labor market frictions raise a country's welfare, such reductions may reduce or raise its rate of unemployment. And finally, reductions in a country's labor market frictions negatively impact its trade partner in terms of productivity and welfare, yet coordinated reductions in labor market frictions in both countries benefit them both. The last observation is of particular interest for evaluating policies, such as the drive to improve labor market flexibility in some European Union countries but not necessarily in all.

So far I have assumed that all workers are identical, and this has led to equal wage payments to all workers in a given sector. In particular, in the differentiated-product sector, firms with different productivity levels paid the same wages. In the remainder of this chapter I examine the impact of trade on inequality when workers are paid different wages in the same sector. In Chapter 3 we discussed the impact of trade on different factors of production, such as capital and labor, or skilled and unskilled workers. Here we focus instead on differential impacts of trade on workers with similar characteristics (i.e., on within-group inequality). This discussion is based on Helpman, Itskhoki, and Redding (2010a). The interest in the impact of trade on wage inequality arises for two main reasons. First, it has been documented by labor economists that wage inequality is large among workers with similar characteristics,[121] and it is of interest to know whether trade contributes to this type of wage dispersion. Second, the observed rise of wage inequality in the 1980s and early 1990s encompassed developed and developing countries alike.[122] As a result, when examining this evidence through the lens of the factor proportions theory, it is difficult to attach a large role to trade liberalization in the rise of wage inequality, because this theory predicts opposing shifts in wage inequality in developed and developing countries in response to trade liberalization. If, however, trade liberalization were to raise wage inequality within groups of similar workers, one could potentially explain these data.[123]

Helpman, Itskhoki, and Redding (2010a) extend the analytical framework of Helpman and Itskhoki (2010) in several directions to examine the link between international trade and wage inequality within groups of similar workers. In particular, they introduce match-specific productivity differences across firms and workers. They consider a setup in which workers are identical ex-ante. Once a worker is matched with a firm, however, the fit of the worker to the job is randomly realized, and this fit varies across workers. Moreover, the quality of this match-specific relationship is not observable unless the firm spends resources on screening its potential employees. The incentive to bear the cost of screening is particularly strong when complementarities exist between the workers' abilities. That is, the marginal contribution of a worker to the firm's output is larger the larger the average ability of the firm's entire labor force is. Under these circumstances, firms are willing to invest resources in screening, even if the screening process provides only partial information about a worker's match-specific productivity. As a result, firms that are more productive invest more in screening, employ workers with higher average ability, and pay them higher wages.

This theory predicts wage dispersion across workers with similar characteristics and what is known as a "size-wage premium" (i.e., higher wages paid by larger and more-productive firms), consistent with the evidence (see Oi and Idson, 1999). Moreover, since larger and more-productive firms export, while smaller and less-productive firms do not, it predicts that exporters pay higher wages than nonexporters, also consistent with the evidence (see Bernard and Jensen, 1995, 1999, and Bernard, Jensen, Redding, and Schott, 2007).

In this economic environment trade raises wage inequality within every industry. More precisely, it raises wage inequality if only a fraction of firms export when the country engages in foreign trade. On the other hand, starting from a trade regime, partial trade liberalization may increase or reduce wage inequality within an industry; wage inequality rises when only a small fraction of firms export—which is the empirically more relevant case—and it can fall when a large fraction of firms export. While the relationship between trade liberalization and wage inequality

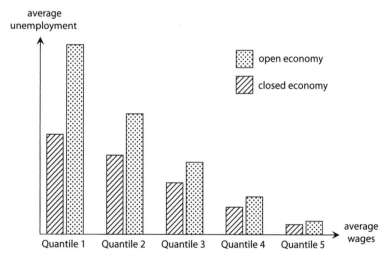

Figure 5.4. Unemployment vs. wages in autarky and in a trade equilibrium.

need not be monotonic, it can be, in which case trade liberalization can increase wage inequality in all countries. Whether this is only a theoretical possibility or an empirically relevant finding is as yet unknown.

Another interesting implication is that trade impacts differently workers with matches of different quality. The average wage within a group of workers with a similar match quality is higher the better the quality of the matches is.[124] In addition, the average unemployment within a group of workers with a similar match quality is higher the lower the quality of the matches. As a result, if the wage distribution is used to divide workers into equal groups of similar earners, say into quantiles (five equally sized groups), and the groups are ordered by average wages, then the average rate of unemployment declines across these quantiles, consistent with the evidence (see Juhn, Murphy, and Topel, 1991). This type of relationship holds both in autarky and in a trade regime. However, in the trade regime there is more dispersion; unemployment rises faster as one moves from a quantile of higher earners to a quantile of lower earners, as illustrated in Figure 5.4.[125]

We have examined in this chapter the impact of trade on reallocations within industries that are populated by firms with different productivities. This theory has been designed to match a variety of findings in empirical studies, and it yields new insights into trade, productivity, unemployment, and inequality. While rich in detail, the analysis has so far been limited to firms that choose strategically whether to serve only the domestic market or also to export, but these firms were not allowed to acquire subsidiaries in foreign countries. Because the multinational activities of business firms have increased in importance in recent decades, not only in the form of trade but also in the form of foreign direct investment and off-shoring more generally, the next chapter discusses the impact on specialization and interdependence of more complex forms of the international organization of production.

6

Offshoring and Outsourcing

Despite their richness, the analytical frameworks discussed in the previous chapters miss elements of the international organization of production that have grown in prominence in recent decades. In particular, fragmentation of the production process across firms and countries is more prevalent now than ever before, and this has affected the sourcing strategies of corporations at home and abroad. The proximate cause of these changes has been developments in information technology (IT), which greatly improved communications, computer-aided design, and computer-aided manufacturing. These improvements enable producers to split the production process into stages that can be physically and geographically separated from each other and located in different regions of the same country or in different countries.

To accommodate these new technological possibilities in a cost-effective way, business firms have changed their organizational forms and management practices.[126] In particular, the outsourcing of various stages of production, to both domestic and foreign suppliers, has increased substantially, and these practices have spread across many industries in the

United States.[127] To avoid confusion, I use the term "outsourcing" to refer to the acquisition of goods or services from an unaffiliated party (i.e., from a company that neither owns nor is owned by the buyer of the goods or services), and independently of whether the unaffiliated supplier is located at home or abroad. And I use the term "offshoring" to refer to the sourcing of a good or service in a foreign country, either from an affiliated or an unaffiliated supplier. According to the latter definition, the offshoring of various stages of production, and especially the production of intermediate inputs, has increased rapidly, greatly expanding world trade. Feenstra and Hanson (1996b) find, for example, that between 1972 and 1990 the share of imports in the total purchase of intermediate inputs by U.S. firms more than doubled, from 5 percent to 11.6 percent, and Campa and Goldberg (1997) report similar trends in Canada and the United Kingdom.[128]

Foreign direct investment (FDI) by multinational companies has grown faster than world trade, exceeding $1.8 trillion in 2007.[129] Like trade in goods and services, FDI flows primarily across developed countries. The total outflow of FDI from developed economies in 2007 amounted to 85 percent of world FDI outflows, and more than $1.2 trillion of these investments poured into developed economies.[130] But FDI is a financial measure that does not necessarily provide a good approximation to the involvement of multinational corporations in the world economy.[131] Other measures, such as output, employment, and trade, also show the importance of multinational corporations. According to Bernard, Jensen, and Schott (2009), in their sample of (approximately) 5.5 million U.S. firms in 2000, about 1.1 percent were multinationals that engaged in foreign trade. These firms employed more than 31 million workers, accounting for 27.4 percent of total civilian employment in the United States. Moreover, they controlled 90 percent of U.S. imports and a slightly higher fraction of U.S. exports. On the import side, about half of U.S. trade in 2000 was intrafirm (i.e., trade among affiliated parties),[132] while on the export side, intrafirm trade was a little less than one-third.[133] Evidently, U.S. multinationals play a big role in employment and foreign trade.

To understand the complex and changing pattern of trade flows, it is necessary to understand why some firms export while others supply foreign markets via foreign subsidiaries; why some firms offshore parts of their value chain while others do not; and why, among those who offshore, some use arm's-length suppliers while others use affiliated suppliers. In other words, we need to understand why some firms choose to outsource fragments of production while others choose integration, and when they choose either outsourcing or integration why some choose to stay at home while others go abroad. When a car manufacturer outsources at home the supply of a component, such as a car engine, this decision does not affect foreign trade directly.[134] But if instead the carmaker outsources the supply of engines to a foreign country, this impacts foreign trade directly, and these imports are viewed as arm's-length trade. On the other hand, if the car manufacturer produces its own engines, then it still needs to decide whether to produce them at home or in a foreign country. If it produces the engines at home, it does not impact foreign trade directly. But if it constructs a plant of its own in a foreign country, manufactures the engines there, and imports them back to its assembly plant at home, then it impacts the home country's imports directly. Moreover, these imports are documented as intrafirm trade.

Foreign trade is influenced in additional ways when the car manufacturer that builds its own engines sells some of them to other car manufacturers as well. When the engines are produced in the home country and some are sold to foreign carmakers, these sales contribute directly to the home country's exports. Alternatively, when the engines are produced in a foreign country and shipped home for the parent company's use or for sale to other car manufacturers in the home country, these shipments raise the home country's imports; the former raise intrafirm trade while the latter raise arm's-length trade. And the foreign subsidiary can also export engines to car manufacturers in third countries (countries in which the parent firm is not located), thus contributing to the host country's exports.

Evidently, foreign direct investment can feed foreign trade in complicated ways, making trade and FDI interdependent. On the one hand, patterns of FDI influence patterns of trade. On the other hand, the profitability of different forms of FDI depends on the profitability of various trade options. As a result, firms' choices of multinational integration strategies depend on trading opportunities. Under the circumstances, trade and FDI become inseparable twins.

6.1 Offshoring

The secular rise in the wages of skilled workers relative to the unskilled, from the late 1970s to the mid-1990s, triggered a debate concerning the causes of this change. This relative wage increased most dramatically in the United States, but it also increased in other OECD countries, and in particular in the United Kingdom and New Zealand. Yet this was not only a rich-country phenomenon; this shift also occurred in less-developed countries. As a result, income disparity widened in many parts of the world.

On one side of the debate were scholars who argued that globalization, in the form of expanding participation of less-developed countries in foreign trade, was responsible for this outcome. On the other side were scholars who argued that globalization played a limited role and that technological change was the main culprit. The interested reader can find in Helpman (2004, chapter 6) a review of this debate. Since offshoring was proposed as a contributor to this evolution of relative wages, I discuss here the ways in which offshoring can impact relative wages.

Feenstra and Hanson (1996a) suggest that foreign direct investment flows from a rich to a poor country can lead to rising wage inequality in both. They observe that a modern production process requires many intermediate inputs (or stages of production) to manufacture a final good. These intermediate inputs differ in factor intensity. Some, such as design, are high-skill–intensive; others, such as assembly, are low-skill–intensive. When factor prices differ between a rich and a poor country, the relative wage of the skilled workers is higher in the rich country. As a result, if it pays to shift the production of intermediate inputs from the rich to the poor country, it is particularly cost effective to shift the most low-skill–intensive parts of the value chain. Because the least skill-intensive activities in the rich country can be more skill-intensive than the most skill-intensive activities in the poor country, a strategy of rich-country firms to source their least skill-intensive intermediates in the poor country raises the relative demand for skilled workers in both countries, and this raises in turn the relative wage of skilled workers in both. Note that this argument does not require FDI; it only requires rich-country firms to acquire low-skill–intensive intermediates in the poor country, from subsidiaries or at arm's-length.[135]

To examine the empirical plausibility of this mechanism, Feenstra and Hanson (1997) study the impact of U.S. foreign direct investment in Mexican maquiladoras, which are assembly plants designated for exports. Such plants typically import inputs from the United States, assemble them into final products, and ship these products back to the United States. Feenstra and Hanson find that FDI of U.S. firms in the maquiladoras is positively correlated with the rise of the share of skilled labor in Mexico's wage bill. Moreover, in regions with the highest concentration of FDI, their estimates account for about half the growth of this wage share during the 1980s.

A more refined theory of the offshoring of parts of the value chain is developed by Grossman and Rossi-Hansberg (2008). They envision a production process that consists of tasks, and a variety of tasks have to be performed in order to manufacture a final product. Some of these tasks are skilled-labor–intensive, while others are unskilled-labor–intensive. Every task can be performed in the firm's home country or abroad, but because of transportation and communication costs it is more expensive—not accounting for factor price differences—to send a task offshore. Under these circumstances a firm has to weigh the cost of offshoring against the potential cost saving from performing a task in a foreign country where unskilled workers receive low wages (such as China or India).

Of particular interest is their analysis of the case in which it is prohibitively costly to offshore high-skill–intensive tasks and the cost of offshoring low-skill–intensive tasks varies across tasks; that is, some tasks are more expensive to offshore than others. Under these circumstances the best strategy is to offshore all the tasks whose offshoring cost is below a cutoff, and to locate in the home country all the tasks above this cutoff. At the cutoff, the firm is indifferent between locating the task at home or abroad.

Grossman and Rossi-Hansberg consider the impact of a proportional decline in the cost of offshoring unskilled-labor–intensive tasks, showing that it can be decomposed into three effects: a productivity effect, a relative-price effect, and a labor-supply effect. When the cost of offshoring falls, more tasks are offshored, leading to more efficient use of low-skilled workers in the home country. This creates a novel effect that is similar to an increase in the productivity of low-skilled workers (i.e., a productivity effect). The other two effects are more conventional. The relative-price effect arises when lower offshoring costs lead to a mismatch between world demand and world supply of products at the original prices, leading to price adjustments that clear markets. And the labor-supply effect arises for the reason that lower offshoring costs reduce the demand for low-skilled workers who perform the low-skill–intensive tasks in the home country, because some of the tasks that were originally performed there are offshored. As a result, more labor is available for other uses.

In situations in which relative prices do not change (e.g., when the home country is small) and the labor-supply effect does not change factor prices (e.g., when production is similar to a two-sector, two-factor

Heckscher-Ohlin environment), only the productivity effect remains. Since in this case lower offshoring costs raise the productivity of unskilled workers and no other pressure on factor prices exists, the result is that the wage of the unskilled workers rises and the wage of the skilled workers does not change, so that the relative wage of the unskilled *rises*. Evidently, there are plausible circumstances in which offshoring jobs of low-skilled workers benefits rather than harms them. This impact of offshoring on relative wages is just the opposite of Feenstra and Hanson's result. It is clear from this analysis that many details of an offshoring process are needed in order to assess its impact on wages.

6.2 The Traditional Approach

Traditional studies of multinational corporations used Dunning's (1977) eclectic approach, which argues that a company needs to have advantages in three areas in order to form a subsidiary in a foreign country: ownership, location, and internalization. This is often referred to as the OLI approach. According to this view, a firm can attain an ownership advantage by possessing specific assets, such as the technology to produce a differentiated product, or by operating in an industry in which certain overhead costs can be shared between parent and subsidiary. There also needs to be some advantage in locating a plant or a servicing subsidiary in a foreign country, which may stem from low production costs in the host country, savings of transport costs, or a competitive advantage from marketing or servicing the product in the host country's consumer market. Finally, there has to be an advantage to retaining control of the subsidiary instead of using alternative arrangements, such as licensing the production or distribution of the product to other firms in the host country. For example, it might be hard to save on overhead costs when the good is produced by a nonaffiliated party, or the firm may not be able to secure the propriety of its technology if it makes the technology available to an independent entity. Evidently, the OLI approach can accommodate a wide variety of specific factors in explaining FDI patterns. But it is, in a sense, too broad for the construction of a theory with sharp predictions.

In answering his critics, Dunning (1988) acknowledges the broad-brush nature of his approach, stating, "It is accepted that, precisely because of its generality, the eclectic paradigm has only limited power to explain or predict particular kinds of international production; and even less, the behaviour of individual enterprises" (p. 1). He goes on to compare the OLI approach to the neoclassical theory of international trade, and particularly, to the factor proportions theory, with no trade frictions. He states:

> The difference between the neo-technology and other modern theories of trade and those of international production is that, while the former *implicitly* assume that all goods are exchanged between independent buyers and sellers across national frontiers, the latter *explicitly* postulate that the transfer of intermediate products is undertaken within the same enterprises. In other words, without international market failure, the raison d'être for international production disappears. But once it exists, explanations of trade and production may be thought of as a part of a general paradigm based upon the international disposition of factor endowments, and the costs of alternative modalities for transacting intermediate products across national boundaries. (p. 2)

Dunning (1988) also comments approvingly on the attempts in the 1980s to develop more detailed models of foreign trade and FDI, such as the work of Helpman (1984b) on vertical FDI, Markusen (1984) on horizontal FDI, and Ethier (1986) on FDI with explicit treatment of the internalization decision.[136]

The distinction between vertical and horizontal FDI is at the core of the traditional literature, and this distinction is useful up to a point. A subsidiary in a foreign country represents pure vertical FDI when it engages in activities that differ from those of the parent firm at home, and it represents pure horizontal FDI when it engages in the same activities as the parent firm at home. An example of pure vertical FDI would be the construction of a plant for the manufacturing of engines in a foreign country, with the engines being exclusively used by the parent car manufacturer. And an example of pure horizontal FDI would be the construction of an integrated plant for the manufacturing of cars in a foreign country, with its cars being exclusively sold in the host country. However, the distinction between horizontal and vertical FDI has become less useful over time, because now multinationals employ much more complicated patterns of FDI than ever before, as illustrated by the prior discussion. UNCTAD (1998) has dubbed them "complex integration strategies." Many of the large multinationals engage in both horizontal and vertical foreign direct investment, as well as in "platform" FDI (i.e., investment in subsidiaries for export purposes).[137] Moreover, various forms of FDI are interdependent. For example, a decision to engage in horizontal FDI often cannot be divorced from a decision to engage in vertical FDI. For this reason I discuss horizontal FDI in the next section, vertical FDI in the following section, and complex integration in section 6.5.[138] In the last section of this chapter, I discuss the internalization decision regarding various stages of production and how it impacts international trade among affiliated entities of the same business firm.

6.3 Horizontal FDI

Consider the acquisition of a subsidiary in a foreign country, whose purpose is to serve the host country's market (i.e., the country that hosts the subsidiary). As such, this type of FDI is motivated by market access considerations, and it serves as a substitute for exports. For example, a Japanese car manufacturer can serve the U.S. market with exports from Japan, or it can build plants in the United States and manufacture cars in these plants for sale in the United States. Which mode of operation is more profitable depends on a host of factors, including the cost of shipping cars from Japan to the United States, the cost of building plants in the United States, and the expected sales in the U.S. market. The first two of these factors represents the proximity-concentration tradeoff; that is, the tradeoff between saving the shipping costs by investing in the United States, and saving the costs of acquiring plants in the U.S. market by exporting. In other words, proximity to the customers saves costs of exporting while concentration of production in the parent country saves fixed investment costs.

Figure 6.1 illustrates the proximity-concentration tradeoff for the product of a particular firm.[139] On the horizontal axis we measure the size of the host country's market for this product, that is, whether its demand is high or low. Both profits from exporting and profits from FDI are increasing in market size, as shown by the profit curves. Every point on a profit curve represents the highest profit the firm can attain when it chooses the mode of serving the foreign market represented by this curve (i.e., exports or subsidiary sales). The figure is drawn under the assumption that there are no fixed export costs, and therefore the export profit curve starts at the origin, while there is a fixed cost of subsidiary sales, and

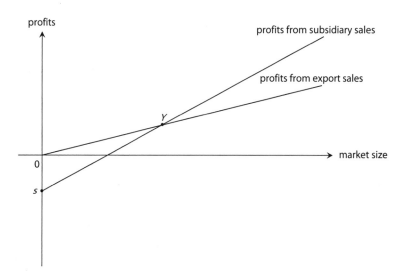

Figure 6.1. FDI: The Proximity-Concentration Tradeoff.

therefore the profit curve for subsidiary sales starts below the horizontal axis.[140] The distance from the horizontal axis to point s represents the size of the fixed cost of subsidiary sales. This fixed cost represents the cost of acquiring plants in the host country, plus any additional costs for serving the foreign market, such as licensing or the formation of a servicing network. The fixed cost of export is assumed to equal zero only for simplicity; what is important for the following arguments is that the fixed cost of FDI exceeds the fixed cost of exporting, which gives an advantage to the concentration of production.

A second feature of the figure is that the slope of the FDI profit curve is steeper than the slope of the export profit curve. This difference in slopes represents the advantage of proximity to the destination market, and it results from the fact that there are variable costs of exporting. These costs consist of freight charges, insurance, and possible trade impediments in the destination country, such as tariffs or nontariff barriers to trade. They apply per unit of exports, so that they represent variable trade costs. Naturally, manufacturing costs in the parent and host countries also influence the difference in the slopes of these profit curves; for example, the higher wages are in the host country the flatter is the profit curve for subsidiary sales, and the higher wages are in the parent country the flatter is the profit curve for exporting. We shall discuss such cost differences in the next section, and assume for the time being that the difference in the slopes of the profit curves arises from differences in variable trade costs.

It is evident from this figure that exports are more profitable than subsidiary sales for demand levels to the left of the intersection point Y, while subsidiary sales are more profitable for higher demand levels. Therefore we should expect more subsidiary sales in countries with larger markets for this product. Moreover, in sectors with higher fixed costs of FDI, the profit curve for subsidiary sales is lower, in which case the intersection point Y is at a higher demand level, implying that we should expect fewer subsidiary sales in such markets. Finally, in sectors with higher variable export costs the export profit curve is flatter, as a result of which the intersection point Y is at a lower demand level, implying that we should expect more subsidiary sales in these sectors. In short, higher impediments to trade raise the profitability of subsidiary sales relative to exporting, while higher fixed costs of FDI raise the profitability of exporting relative to subsidiary sales. This tradeoff is nicely illustrated by Japanese car manufacturers, such as Toyota, who used to export cars to the United States before the 1973 oil crisis, but who invested in manufacturing facilities in the United States after 1973 in response to the United States' protection of its car market.[141] This sort of "tariff jumping" is a well-recognized feature of the proximity-concentration tradeoff.

The insights from these theoretical arguments are used by Brainard (1997) to examine the impact of variable trade costs and fixed costs of FDI on the level of exports relative to subsidiary sales of U.S.-based companies to 27 foreign countries. Using disaggregated data for 1989, Brainard shows that U.S. companies export more relative to subsidiary sales in industries with high fixed costs, and they export less relative to subsidiary sales in industries with high freight charges and high foreign tariffs. Apparently, the main predictions of the market access arguments for horizontal FDI are borne out by these data. Although Brainard did not examine the impact of market size on exports relative to subsidiary sales, this relationship is examined with similar data by Yeaple (2003b). In addition to confirming Brainard's findings that higher FDI fixed costs and lower variable trade impediments raise exports relative to subsidiary sales, Yeaple finds a negative effect of market size on this ratio; that is, exports relative to subsidiary sales are lower in larger markets.[142] Finally, Brainard examines the impact of differences in income per capita between the destination countries and the United States and finds no significant effect of these differences on sectoral exports relative to subsidiary sales. She interprets this finding as evidence against the view that cross-country differences in factor rewards impact the choice between exports and FDI. We shall discuss this finding in the next section.

Brainard's (1997) study, as well as Markusen's (1984) original work on horizontal FDI, use analytical frameworks in which there is no firm heterogeneity within industries. As a result, all firms make the same choices; either all choose to export or all choose to serve a foreign market with subsidiary sales. Under the circumstances FDI cannot coexist with exports in the same industry. Naturally, in interpreting the evidence or in formulating an equation for estimation purposes, this extreme outcome is not taken at face value. Instead, the impacts of the variables that determine the proximity-concentration tradeoff are interpreted as empirical tendencies rather than strict predictions. For example, a rise in the variable export cost is interpreted as making FDI more likely and exports less likely, leading to more subsidiary sales relative to exports. For this statement to be strictly true, however, some heterogeneity is required to enable differences in firm characteristics to induce some to export and others to invest abroad. With firm heterogeneity, a rise in the variable export cost can impel more firms to invest in subsidiaries and fewer to export.

This idea is developed in Helpman, Melitz, and Yeaple (2004). In their framework, firms differ by productivity, as in Melitz (2003).[143] By allowing firms to serve foreign markets with both exports and subsidiary sales, they generate three categories of firms: those that serve only the domestic market, those that export, and those that invest in subsidiaries. Figure 6.2, which is an extension of Figure 5.1, illustrates the selection of firms into these organizational modes. Productivity is measured on the horizontal axis while profits are measured on the vertical axis. In addition to the profit curves for domestic sales and exports, which are taken from Figure 5.1, we have added a profit curve for subsidiary sales. The latter profit curve has two notable features when compared with the export profit curve: it has a lower intercept (point s is below point x) and it is steeper. The lower intercept reflects a higher fixed cost of FDI than exporting, and the steeper slope reflects the fact that exports have variable trade costs while subsidiary sales do not. Naturally, the difference in these slopes also represents differences in unit manufacturing costs between

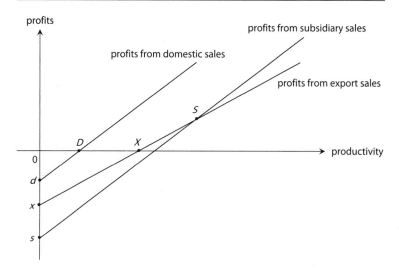

Figure 6.2. Selection into Exports and Subsidiary Sales.

the parent and host countries; if these costs are the same or lower in the host country, the subsidiary sales profit curve is necessarily steeper. But if, for example, wages are higher in the host country, then the profit curve for subsidiary sales is steeper only if the higher unit cost of manufacturing in the host country is not too large relative to the variable export costs. Note, however, that if the fixed cost of FDI is higher than the fixed cost of exporting and the profit curve for exports is steeper, then the profit curve for subsidiary sales is everywhere below the profit curve for exports, in which case every firm, no matter how productive, makes more money from exporting than from subsidiary sales, and therefore there can be no FDI in this industry. In other words, for FDI to exist, the profit curve for subsidiary sales has to be steeper, as depicted in the figure.

In this figure, profit-maximizing firms sort as follows: the lowest-productivity firms, with productivity to the left of point D, leave the industry because they lose money; those with productivity between points D and X serve only the domestic market; firms with productivity between points X and S export and serve the domestic market; and those with productivity to the right of S invest in foreign subsidiaries and serve the domestic market. Evidently, this sorting pattern generates a hierarchy of organizational forms, in which the least-productive firms are domestically oriented, the most-productive firms serve the foreign market with subsidiary sales, and firms with intermediate productivity levels serve foreign markets with exports. This implies that domestic firms have the lowest average productivity, exporters have a higher average productivity, and firms engaged in foreign direct investment have the highest productivity. Indeed, this pattern is consistent with various data sets. Helpman, Melitz, and Yeaple (2004) report, for example, that the average labor productivity (output per worker) of U.S. exporters exceeds the average labor productivity of U.S. domestic firms (which neither export nor invest in foreign countries) by close to 40 percent, while the average labor productivity of firms that engage in FDI exceeds the average labor productivity of exporters by 15 percent. Similar pecking orders are reported by Head and Ries (2003) and Tomiura (2007) for Japan; Girma, Görg, and Strobl (2004) for Ireland; and Girma, Kneller, and Pisu (2005) for the United Kingdom.[144]

Since in this analytical model exporters coexist with foreign direct investors in the same industry, it is possible to calculate the ratio of exports to subsidiary sales by aggregating the export value of all firms with productivities in the range from X to S and by aggregating the subsidiary-sales value of all firms with higher productivity levels. This ratio should be lower the larger the variable trade costs are and the smaller the fixed costs of FDI are, in line with the proximity-concentration tradeoff. In addition, the level of exports relative to subsidiary sales should be smaller the more dispersed the productivity of firms is in the industry, a new prediction that results from the heterogeneity of firms. In other words, the degree of firm heterogeneity has implications for comparative advantage. A natural question is whether this theoretical prediction is borne out by the data, and if it is, whether it is quantitatively important. Helpman,

Melitz, and Yeaple (2004) provide estimates of these effects, in combination with estimates of the effects of variable trade costs and fixed costs of plants on the ratio of exports to subsidiary sales. Table 6.1 reports the standardized form of these estimates, known as "beta" coefficients, which are comparable to each other. These estimates have been obtained from 1994 data on U.S. exports and subsidiary sales in 52 sectors to the 27 countries studied by Brainard (1997).[145] In addition to freight, tariffs, and fixed costs, which are suggested by the proximity-concentration tradeoff, the table reports the impact of different measures of dispersion: the standard deviation of productivity of U.S. firms (U.S. s.d.), the standard deviation of productivity of European firms (Europe s.d.), and the estimated shape parameter of a Pareto distribution from data on European firms (Europe shape).[146] Each one of these measures was estimated for each of the 52 sectors, and they reveal substantial variation across sectors. The table shows that this cross-sectoral variation has a measurable impact on the variation across sectors of the ratio of exports to subsidiary sales. It is indeed evident from the table that the quantitative impact of these dispersion measures on the ratio of exports to subsidiary sales is comparable to freight costs, tariffs, and plant fixed costs.

Yeaple (2009) studies additional implications. He shows that more-productive U.S. multinationals own affiliates in more foreign countries, and they have higher revenues in the host countries the more productive

Table 6.1. Productivity Dispersion and Exports Relative to Subsidiary Sales

	Freight	Tariff	Fixed cost	U.S. s.d.	Europe s.d.	Europe shape
"Beta" coefficients	−0.271	−0.205	0.325	−0.312	−0.250	0.211

Source: Helpman, Melitz, and Yeaple (2004).

Note: The table reports standardized (or "beta") regression coefficients, estimated from regressing the ratio of exports to subsidiary sales on the variables reported in the table, and controlling for sectoral capital-labor ratios and research and development intensity.

they are. Moreover, countries with higher income per capita are more attractive locations for U.S. multinationals, but this is not because they offer lower FDI costs but rather because they offer larger markets (recall the analysis in Figure 6.1, which shows that larger markets make FDI more attractive relative to exports). Finally, Yeaple shows that countries that are more attractive to FDI draw in at the margin smaller and less-productive U.S. multinationals, which reduces the average productivity of their American parent firms.

6.4 Vertical FDI

In the previous section we discussed explanations of horizontal FDI and evidence in their support. These explanations focus on the proximity-concentration tradeoff that arises when a firm seeks market access in a foreign country via either export or subsidiary sales. In that discussion, we assumed that in the case of subsidiary sales the entire value chain is located in the host country, and in the export case the entire value chain is located in the source county. As Markusen (2002, p. 5) describes it: "Horizontal direct investment refers to foreign production of products and services roughly similar to those the firm produces for its home market." And he distinguishes this form of FDI from vertical FDI: "Vertical investments refer to those that geographically fragment the production process by stages of production," by which he means that some stages of production are performed in the host country while others are preformed in the parent country.

Helpman (1984b) proposed an extension of the Helpman-Krugman trade model—which combines factor proportions with product differentiation—to accommodate vertical FDI. The production process in the differentiated sector is decomposed into manufacturing and headquarter services, where the latter includes activities such as management, design, and research and development (R&D). Factor intensities differ across these activities, with headquarter services being more skill-intensive or more capital-intensive than on-the-floor production. Moreover, headquarter services can be shared by a number of manufacturing plants, even when these plants are located in different countries. As a result, a firm in, say, a capital-rich country has an incentive to locate headquarters at home and manufacturing in a labor-rich country when wages of low-skilled workers are lower in the latter. This type of separation of manufacturing from the parent firm's headquarters fits into the definition of vertical FDI. When differences in factor composition are not too large, there is no incentive to go multinational because factor prices are the same in every country. However, when these differences are large, there is incipient pressure for factor prices to differ. Then firms based in the capital-rich country build manufacturing facilities for final goods in the labor-abundant country.

This reallocation of production has implications for the structure of trade. Although it does not affect the qualitative predictions of the factor content of net trade flows,[147] it changes the direction of trade flows in final goods and the share of intra-industry trade. In particular, because manufacturing is shifted abroad, the capital-rich country imports capital-intensive goods—whose final assembly has taken place in the labor-abundant country—when the gap in the two countries' capital-labor ratios is large. And although in the absence of multinational corporations the share of intra-industry trade is smaller the larger the difference is in factor composition between the two countries, this relationship is more nuanced when the differences in factor composition are large enough for multinationals to form. With vertical FDI, the share of intra-industry trade is *larger* the more the countries differ in relative factor endowments—holding constant relative country size—as long as the capital-rich country exports differentiated products on net. Yet when the difference in factor composition is sufficiently large, enough production of final differentiated products takes place in the labor-abundant country to turn the capital-rich country into a net importer of differentiated products. Once this shift in the pattern of trade emerges, the negative relationship between differences in factor composition and the share of intra-industry trade is restored. Evidently, vertical FDI leads to a non-monotonic relationship between the difference in factor composition and the share of intra-industry trade.

The appearance of vertical FDI leads also to intrafirm trade, as the parent firms import final goods from their subsidiaries. The share of these imports in total trade rises with differences in factor composition between the countries, as long as the relative size of the two countries does not change. In other words, the model predicts a positive correlation between the share of intrafirm trade and differences in factor composition across countries.

In this model, parent firms export headquarter services to their subsidiaries and import final products from their subsidiaries. Naturally, parent firms can export headquarter services to subsidiaries even if the subsidiaries produce final goods for sale in their own (i.e., the host) country. When this happens, subsidiary sales reflect horizontal FDI, while the flow of headquarter services attests to vertical FDI. Indeed, in many instances the two forms of FDI are interrelated. For now, however, let us remain in the realm of pure vertical FDI. In this context note that parent firms export intermediate inputs to their subsidiaries, in addition to headquarter services, which the subsidiaries use to produce final goods. Such imports manifest vertical FDI (independently of where the subsidiaries sell their output). And a measure of these intrafirm trade flows is often used to gauge the importance of vertical FDI.

Hanson, Mataloni, and Slaughter (2001, table 6) show, for example, that among majority-owned U.S. multinationals in the manufacturing sector, affiliate imports of goods for further processing increased from close to 10 percent of affiliate sales in 1982 to over 12 percent in 1994, which they interpret as a rise in the relative importance of vertical FDI. This growth was particularly important in certain host countries and certain industries. For U.S. investment in Canada, this share increased from

21.6 percent in 1982 to 33.5 percent in 1994, and for U.S. investment in Mexico, it increased from 18.3 percent to 36.7 percent. At the industry level, it increased from 16.3 percent in 1982 to 22.2 percent in 1994 in the electronic and other electric equipment industry, and from 17.7 percent to 23.2 percent in the transportation equipment industry. Citing a study of the Council on Foreign Relations (2002), Hanson, Mataloni, and Slaughter (2005, p. 664) state that "Canadian and Mexican auto plants have extensive intrafirm links with their U.S. counterparts, mediated by large flows of inputs across borders. It is estimated that every day $250 million in autos and auto parts crosses the Ambassador Bridge that connects Detroit, Michigan with Windsor, Ontario. When the U.S. government closed this bridge and other entry points after the terrorist attacks of September 11, 2001, several NAFTA auto plants had to shut down within 48 hours because of input shortages." They go on to show that the export of intermediate inputs from U.S. parents to their foreign affiliates is sensitive to trade costs and wages in the host countries. In particular, higher trade costs and higher wages of low-skilled workers reduce imports of intermediate inputs from parent firms, while higher wages of high-skilled workers increase them. The results on the impact of wages are particularly interesting, because they suggest that low-skilled workers complement the use of imported intermediates, while high-skilled workers substitute for them.

Horizontal and vertical FDI have been extensively studied because both are important in the data. Brainard's (1997) empirical finding that FDI flows are not correlated with differences in relative factor abundance was interpreted as evidence that the dominant form of FDI is horizontal. On the other side, as already discussed, direct evidence of a growing role for vertical FDI is mounting. So the question is "How can these different pieces of evidence be reconciled?" The best answer to this question is provided by Yeaple (2003b). He first points out that Brainard estimated the *average* impact of cross-country differences in factor composition on the sectoral structure of FDI. However, even if these average effects are not particularly significant, they do not provide a good test of the role of factor endowments in shaping FDI. The reason is that sectors differ by factor intensity, and therefore one needs to ask whether U.S. multinationals invest in high-skill–intensive industries in countries that have an abundance of high-skilled workers and in low-skill–intensive industries in countries that have an abundance of low-skilled workers. If they do, then this provides evidence that U.S. multinationals invest according to the comparative advantage of the host countries, in line with the vertical motive for FDI. In other words, to identify the impact of factor endowments on FDI flows one needs to estimate a model that interacts country characteristics with industry characteristics, similar to the methodology developed by Romalis (2004) for estimating trade flows.

Yeaple's estimates confirm this pattern in the data. He also finds evidence that variable trade costs and fixed costs impact FDI, in line with the proximity-concentration tradeoff, and that market size impacts FDI, in line with the market access hypothesis. In addition, he considers the effect of these variables on exports relative to subsidiary sales. Jointly, the variables that are affiliated with vertical and horizontal FDI explain 22.3 percent of the variance in this ratio.[148] When variables affiliated only with vertical FDI are used for estimation, they explain 13.5 percent of the variance, and when variables affiliated only with horizontal FDI are used, including the market size effect, they explain 14.9 percent of the variance. Judged by these results, both forms of FDI are important for explaining the U.S. data.

6.5 Complex Integration

As the organization of firms in the global economy has become more complex, pure forms of horizontal or vertical FDI cannot provide a satisfactory explanation for the patterns of foreign direct investment. True, subsidiaries of multinational companies sell their products in host countries and import intermediate inputs from parent firms. But they also export products to their parent countries as well as to third markets, to affiliated parties and nonaffiliated parties alike. Blonigen (2005, table 1) reports that in 1999 host-country sales of subsidiaries of U.S. multinationals in manufacturing plus nonmanufacturing sectors exceeded 67 percent of total sales, and the rest was exported. A little over 10 percent of total sales of these firms were sales back to the United States, close to 10 percent were to unaffiliated parties in other foreign countries, and 12.5 percent were to related parties in other foreign countries. In manufacturing, the share of host-country sales was smaller, less than 60 percent, but sales back to the United States were 15 percent, and sales to affiliated parties in other foreign countries exceeded 16 percent.

While these numbers suggest that FDI and trade are related and that this relationship varies across sectors, the data also suggest that this relationship varies across countries. Ekholm, Forslid, and Markusen (2007, table 1) decompose the 2003 sales of U.S. foreign subsidiaries in the manufacturing sector operating in a variety of countries. They report that, while subsidiaries operating in European Union countries sold back little to the United States (between 1 percent and 5 percent of total sales), their sales to third markets varied greatly. For example, Ireland sold 69 percent to third markets, Belgium sold 56 percent, Spain sold 39 percent, and Greece sold only 8 percent. Evidently, Ireland and Belgium served as a large export platform for U.S. multinationals, while in Greece U.S. subsidiaries served mostly the local community (horizontal FDI). Exports back to the United States were much larger from some of the Asian countries, as well as from Canada and Mexico: they were 39 percent from Malaysia, 35 percent from the Philippines, and 15 percent from Hong Kong and Singapore. From Canada and Mexico they were 34 percent and 31 percent, respectively. But they were rather small from Indonesia (2 percent) and China (8 percent). On the other side, export sales from the Asian countries to third countries were large: 43 percent from Singapore; 38 percent from the Philippines; and the smallest, 13 percent, from Indonesia. From Canada, export sales to third countries were only 5 percent, and from Mexico 15 percent.

It is clear from these data that more than one motive drives FDI. While American companies operating in Greece were primarily driven by horizontal FDI considerations, since they exported back to the United States only 1 percent and to third countries only 8 percent of their total sales, in Ireland and Belgium investment was driven primarily by platform FDI. And in Malaysia and the Philippines, both vertical FDI and platform FDI played an important role, where "platform FDI" refers to the acquisition of subsidiaries whose purpose is to export their products to third countries (that is, not to the country in which the parent firm is located).[149] To understand these patterns it is necessary to think about horizontal FDI, vertical FDI, and platform FDI as interrelated strategies.

An important insight into interrelated forms of FDI is provided by Yeaple (2003a). He considers a world of three countries: two Northern developed countries (say the United States and France) and one less-developed Southern country (say the Philippines). Each Northern country consumes a differentiated product that is manufactured by a firm headquartered in a Northern country. To manufacture this good the firm needs two inputs: one is cheaper to produce in the North, the other is cheaper to produce in the South. There are similar transport costs for final and intermediate goods that are proportional to the value of the products. Under these circumstances one can study which one of four strategies is adopted by a Northern firm. First, the firm in, say, the United States may choose to produce both inputs at home and ship assembled goods to France. Second, such a firm may choose to produce one input at home and the other in the Philippines, and ship assembled goods to France (vertical FDI). Third, such a firm may form a subsidiary in France and produce both intermediates at home and in France, and serve each one of the Northern countries with its local producer, the parent firm in the United States and its subsidiary in France (horizontal FDI). Finally, such a firm may choose to produce one component in the Philippines and the other in each one of the Northern countries and, as before, serve each one of the Northern countries with its local producer (complex integration). Yeaple shows how the viability of each one of these options depends on the cost differential of producing intermediate inputs in the North and the South, the shipping cost, and the fixed costs of subsidiaries in the North and the South. He points out that "complex integration strategies create dependence between the level of FDI in one country and the characteristics and policies of its neighbors .... The nature of this dependence can take two forms: two locations may either be complements or substitutes. Two locations are complements when events in one country that expand (contract) MNE activity in that country also expand (contract) MNE activity in the other and are substitutes when events in one country that expand (contract) MNE activity in that country also contract (expand) MNE activity in the other" (p. 295).[150] Whether FDI in the two foreign locations are substitutes or complements depends in this case on the level of transport costs.

For low transport costs, the two forms of FDI tend to be complementary to each other. A firm headquartered in the United States that has a plant in the Philippines that produces intermediate inputs thereby lowers the unit cost of its final good. Under these circumstances, expanding sales should be particularly profitable. One way to expand sales is to form a subsidiary in France to serve the French market. Therefore, a subsidiary in the Philippines makes the subsidiary in France more profitable; and vice versa, a subsidiary in France makes a subsidiary in the Philippines more profitable.

Grossman, Helpman, and Szeidl (2006) modify and extend Yeaple's analysis. Instead of two inputs, they consider a technology in which there is one intermediate input and one assembly activity, each one of which can be located in a different country (the United States, France, or the Philippines). This modification adds the possibility of platform FDI (e.g., assembly in the Philippines with exports to the North). They also allow goods to be consumed in both the North and the South. Moreover, differentiated-product firms are heterogeneous, so that companies with different productivity levels may choose different integration strategies, and the transport costs of final goods may differ from the transport costs of intermediates. In this event some firms may choose to produce intermediates at home, assemble final goods in the home country, and serve foreign countries with exports, while other firms may choose one or more forms of FDI. This heterogeneity in organizational form is present in the data.

This richer analytical framework allows Grossman, Helpman, and Szeidl to study three different forms of complementarity between foreign direct investments, which they term "unit-cost," "source-of-components," and "agglomeration" complementarities, where the unit-cost complementarity is similar to the one identified by Yeaple. They define complementarity as follows (p. 219): "In general, we say that FDI in assembly is complementary to FDI in components when an increase in the fixed cost of assembly abroad reduces the fraction of firms that perform FDI in components, and vice versa, when an increase in the fixed cost of FDI in components reduces the fraction of firms that engage in foreign assembly." Under this definition, unit-cost complementarity exists even in the absence of shipment costs for intermediate inputs and final goods. To see why, first note that in the absence of transport costs, an integrated firm in the United States, which produces intermediates at home and also assembles final goods there, never invests in France, because FDI in France saves no costs but carries fixed FDI costs. More generally, in this case a firm has no reason to do the same activity in multiple locations, because this would raise fixed costs but not save shipment costs. As a result, intermediates are produced in the home country or in the Philippines, and similarly, assembly takes place either in the home country or in the Philippines.

The resulting patterns of FDI are depicted in Figure 6.3, for a given fixed cost of FDI in assembly. Low-productivity firms do not engage in FDI, because they cannot cover the fixed costs. On the other side, very

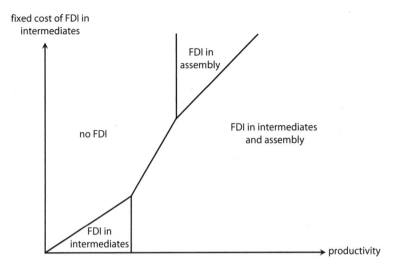

Figure 6.3. Patterns of FDI: no transport costs.

highly productive firms build integrated subsidiaries in the Philippines, which produce intermediates and assemble final products. Therefore the low-productivity firms export their products from the home country, while the very high productivity firms export their products from the Philippines. Evidently, the Philippines are an export platform for the very productive firms; they sell a fraction of their output to residents of the Philippines and export the rest to the United States and France.

Moderately productive firms do not engage in FDI when the fixed cost of FDI in intermediate inputs is high. But when this fixed cost is low enough, they build subsidiaries in the Philippines to manufacture intermediates. These intermediates are then exported back to the home country in the North and assembled there into final products. The final products are sold domestically and exported to the Philippines and to the other Northern country.

Some highly productive firms, which would have acquired integrated facilities for the production of final goods in the Philippines if the fixed cost of FDI in intermediate inputs had been low enough, opt for FDI in assembly only, when the fixed cost of FDI in intermediates is high. These firms produce intermediates in the home country and export them for further processing to the Philippines. In the Philippines, their subsidiaries use the intermediates to assemble final products, which are then exported back to the home country as well as to the other Northern country.

Evidently, these patterns of FDI resemble what we have seen in the data. Moreover, it is apparent from the figure that as the fixed cost of FDI in intermediate inputs rises, a smaller fraction of firms engages in FDI, including FDI in assembly (because the productivity cutoff that makes these activities profitable rises). Hence the unit-cost complementarity between the two forms of FDI: lower costs of intermediates in the Philippines encourage FDI in assembly, and lower unit costs of assembly encourage FDI in intermediates.

When shipping final goods across borders is costly (but intermediates ship costlessly), the patterns of FDI depicted in Figure 6.3 still apply, as long as the transport cost is low enough. Higher transport costs lead to richer patterns of integration. This is due partly to the emergence of a new source of complementarity between the two types of FDI: source-of-components complementarity. It stems from the fact that cost saving from conducting assembly in the Philippines is relatively larger when intermediate inputs are also manufactured in the Philippines, which strengthens the strategic considerations that emanate from the unit-cost complementarity. Unlike the case of no transport costs, however, now there is an incentive for FDI in assembly in the other Northern country, and this incentive is stronger when intermediates are produced at low cost in the Philippines.

When the transport cost of final goods is high and the market in the Philippines is small, an interesting pattern of FDI emerges for low fixed costs of FDI in intermediates. This pattern is illustrated in Figure 6.4. Low-productivity firms operate integrated facilities in the home country and export their final goods to the other Northern country and to the Philippines. Firms with somewhat higher productivity levels manufacture intermediate inputs in the Philippines and import them back home in order to assemble final goods. In this case there is pure vertical FDI and every Northern firm exports final goods both to the other Northern country and to the Philippines. Still higher-productivity firms also manufacture intermediates in the Philippines (i.e., engage in vertical FDI), except that they also acquire subsidiaries in the other Northern country. These subsidiaries assemble final goods from intermediate inputs that are shipped from the firm's affiliate in the Philippines. Note that in this case horizontal FDI in the other Northern country is enabled by the vertical FDI in the South, so that these two forms of FDI are interrelated. There is no U.S.-France trade in final goods, however, but Northern firms serve the Philippines with export of final goods. Also note that the Philippines are an export platform; the intermediates produced there are not used in the Philippines, but rather exported to the United States and France. Finally, the most-productive firms manufacture intermediate inputs in

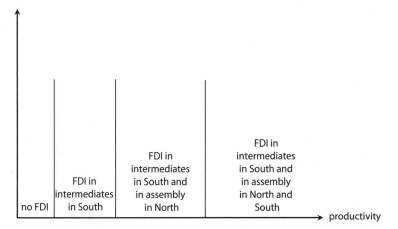

Figure 6.4. Patterns of FDI: High transport cost of final goods, low fixed cost of FDI in intermediate inputs, and small market in the South.

the Philippines and assemble final goods in all three countries. Again, the Philippines are an export platform for intermediates, but a fraction of these intermediates is now used for local assembly, and the final goods thus assembled are sold in the Philippines.

I have demonstrated in this section that complex patterns of FDI can be explained with simple tradeoffs between variable costs, fixed costs, and transport costs. Although this theory has not yet been tested, it predicts patterns of FDI that are consistent with evidence on the operation of U.S. affiliates in foreign countries.

6.6 Internalization

In previous sections, the discussion of multinational corporations did not address the internalization decision; that is, there was no explicit analysis of *why* a firm chooses to serve a foreign market via subsidiary sales, or *why* a firm chooses to produce intermediate inputs in a foreign subsidiary. Naturally, in each of these cases the firm can use a foreign firm that is not its affiliate. For example, the firm can license a foreign company to manufacture final goods for local sales, using the firm's brand name, or it can license a foreign company to manufacture intermediate inputs. So the question is "When does it choose to own the foreign producer?" In similar fashion one can ask "When does a firm choose to own a domestic supplier of parts?" Such integration decisions are relevant for foreign and domestic sourcing alike. As a result, there are multiple organizational forms to choose from, and every firm fashions its own strategy.

To investigate the organizational decisions of business firms and their implications for trade and FDI, scholars have adopted a number of approaches. First, there is the transactions cost analysis of firm boundaries, implicit in Dunning's (1977) eclectic approach.[151] Second, there is the managerial incentives analysis of internalization, used by Grossman and Helpman (2004) and Marin and Verdier (2008a,b).[152] Third, there is the property rights approach to the organization of firms that builds on the theory of incomplete contracts, used by Grossman and Helpman (2002a), Antràs (2003), Antràs and Helpman (2004), and many other more recent studies.[153] In what follows I focus on the third approach, because it provides predictions that were successfully studied with a variety of data sets.

The basic tradeoffs embodied in these studies concern the costs and benefits of internalization. In its simplest form, one can think about two activities that have to be performed to manufacture a final product. One party, say H, owns the technology and the know-how to manufacture the good, and manufacturing requires headquarter services that only H can provide. The other activity has to be performed by a second party, say S, but S can be part of H's enterprise or an independent supplier. Suppose that S has to supply components. Importantly, the components needed by H are highly specialized, so that if S makes them available in the correct specifications, only H can use them; the components have no value outside the relationship between H and S. For this reason, once S manufactures the components, she becomes H's hostage. But if S is the only supplier of these parts, which for simplicity we assume to be the case, then H is also S's hostage, because H cannot manufacture the final goods without S's input. Under the circumstances H and S bargain ex-post for the payment S will receive from H for her components. For this to be the case it is assumed that the two parties cannot sign a detailed contract that specifies the nature of these components in a way that would make the contract enforceable in a court of law, because the specification of the requisite characteristics is very complicated and a judge or a jury would not be able to verify whether the intermediate inputs satisfied them or not.[154]

What is the outcome of the ex-post bargaining? In situations like this the answer depends on the surplus H and S can generate by cooperating with each other and on the value each one of them can derive from his or her assets in case the relationship between them breaks down. That is, it depends on their outside options. If S is an independent supplier, her components have no value outside this relationship, and therefore her outside option equals zero. Similarly for H: if he cannot manufacture the final good without the components, his outside option also equals zero. Given every party's bargaining power, each one gets their outside option—zero, in this case—plus a share of the surplus in accordance with their bargaining power. Moreover, the surplus equals the revenue from sales of final goods minus the outside options of H and S. In the case of outsourcing, this implies that the revenue is divided in proportion to the bargaining power of each party.

In the alternative organizational form, when S is integrated into H's company, H owns the intermediate inputs manufactured by S. In this event S cannot take the intermediate inputs with her if the relationship between her and H breaks down, when she either quits or is dismissed by H. Therefore in this case, as in the case of outsourcing, her outside option equals zero. But for H, integration differs from outsourcing, because under integration H owns the intermediate inputs. Without the supplier, H most likely cannot convert the intermediate inputs and headquarter services into final goods as efficiently as he does with S's cooperation. As a result, he attains a level of revenue that is lower than the revenue attained with S's cooperation. Nonetheless, this lower revenue is now H's outside option in the bargaining game, which is larger than his zero outside option under outsourcing. For this reason H is able to bargain for a higher fraction of the revenue under integration than under outsourcing. This higher fraction is a key advantage of integration for H.

Or is it? It is easy to be misled into thinking that H necessarily prefers an organizational form that gives him a higher fraction of the revenue, because a larger fraction of revenue appears to be preferable to a smaller fraction. This is of course so if the organizational form *does not affect the revenue*, a supposition that is hardly ever true. The reason is that S has less of an incentive to work hard in producing high-quality intermediate inputs if she expects to get a smaller share of the revenue. And similarly,

H has less of an incentive to work hard in producing high-quality headquarter services if he gets a smaller share of the revenue. Shirking or lower investment by either side reduces the available revenue, making the pie to be divided smaller. For this reason, H does not always opt for integration in order to obtain a larger share of the revenue. In particular, if components play an important role relative to headquarter services in the manufacturing of final goods, he may prefer to outsource in order to provide S with strong incentives to invest and work hard. Antràs (2003) shows that there exists a cutoff level of the relative importance of intermediate inputs such that companies with a measure of importance above this cutoff prefer outsourcing and those below it prefer integration.

Antràs (2003) embodies this structure in a two-country, two-sector, two-input model of international trade in which the relative importance of intermediate inputs is measured by a sector's labor intensity. As a result, firms choose outsourcing in the labor-intensive sector and integration in the capital-intensive sector. The model predicts intrafirm trade in the capital-intensive sector and arm's-length trade in the labor-intensive sector. Loosely interpreted, this implies that a country's imports from a capital-rich country should exhibit a larger share of intrafirm trade than its imports from a less capital-rich country. And at the sectoral level, a country's share of intrafirm imports should be larger the more capital-intensive the sector is. Using data on U.S. imports from 28 countries and 23 industries, Antràs finds support for both predictions.[155] Figure 6.5 depicts the relationship between the share of intrafirm trade and the exporting country's capital-labor ratio in 1992.[156] The positive correlation is apparent; the share of intrafirm imports is low from labor-rich countries such as Egypt and Indonesia, and high from capital-rich countries such as Germany and Switzerland.

Antràs's theoretical model implies that sectoral imports are either all intrafirm or all arm's-length, while in the data there is a mix of both. Moreover, the share of intrafirm trade varies across sectors. To accommodate this feature and additional characteristics of trade and FDI, Antràs and

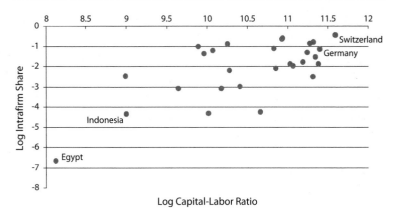

Figure 6.5. U.S. share of intrafirm imports from 28 countries, 1992. Data from Antràs (2003).

Helpman (2004) introduce firm heterogeneity into each sector and fixed costs that vary by organizational form. They assume that the fixed costs are higher for offshore operations than for home activities: outsourcing abroad involves a higher fixed cost than outsourcing at home, and the fixed cost of FDI is higher than the fixed cost of integration at home. They also assume that integration is more costly than outsourcing (i.e., the fixed cost of integration at home is higher than the fixed cost of outsourcing at home and the fixed cost of FDI is higher than the fixed cost of outsourcing offshore). While the first set of assumptions is quite reasonable, the second is harder to defend. The reason is that an integrated firm can save fixed costs if it has economies of scope. That is, the horizontal expansion of a firm's activities saves fixed costs per activity, but an integrated firm imposes a larger burden on management that may raise the fixed cost of the firm's operation. In other words, the fixed cost of integration is not necessarily higher than the fixed cost of outsourcing.[157] Naturally, this theoretical model can be analyzed under each one of these alternative assumptions, and I will point out the differences in implications.

The sorting pattern predicted by Antràs and Helpman (2004) is depicted in Figure 6.6 for the case in which manufacturing costs are lower in the foreign country. As usual in the presence of fixed costs, the least-productive firms exit. Among the surviving firms, those with low productivity source inputs at home and those with high productivity source inputs abroad. Within the group of firms that acquire intermediate inputs onshore, the least productive acquire them via outsourcing while the more productive manufacture them in-house. And within the group of firms that acquire intermediate inputs offshore, the least productive outsource while the more productive integrate; those who outsource import their intermediates at arm's length, while those who integrate import from subsidiaries, that is, they engage in intrafirm trade. As in the model of horizontal FDI, here too the most-productive firms become multinationals.

Reversing the order of fixed costs between integration and outsourcing does not change the prediction that low-productivity firms source inputs onshore and high-productivity firms source inputs offshore. However, when integration has lower fixed costs than outsourcing, lower-productivity firms opt for integration and higher-productivity firms opt for outsourcing at home and abroad. In other words, among the firms that source their inputs at home the least productive integrate and the most productive outsource, while among the firms that offshore the least productive become multinationals and the most productive outsource.

While Figure 6.6 depicts all four organizational forms that can emanate from the 2×2 organizational structure (home vs. foreign, integration vs. outsourcing), it is possible for some bins to be empty in some sectors. For example, in a sector with very low headquarter intensity, a firm would like to give its supplier high-powered incentives, because the components are particularly important in the production process. As a result it will opt for outsourcing no matter how productive it is, because this gives the supplier the best incentives to invest and to exert effort

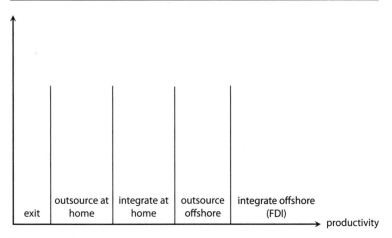

Figure 6.6. Sorting in the Antràs-Helpman model.

and because the fixed cost is lower under outsourcing. Under these circumstances the only question is whether the firm offshores the supply of intermediate inputs. The result is that low-productivity firms choose domestic outsourcing, which saves fixed costs, while high-productivity firms choose foreign outsourcing, which saves variable costs.

Using this sorting pattern, one can characterize the fraction of firms that choose each type of organizational form and their market shares. Antràs and Helpman show that offshoring is higher in sectors with lower headquarter intensity and in sectors with higher productivity dispersion. Moreover, in higher headquarter-intensive sectors, in which the sorting pattern is as depicted in Figure 6.6, there is more integration relative to outsourcing—both at home and abroad—the more headquarter-intensive a sector is or the higher its productivity dispersion is.

Yeaple (2006) uses U.S. firm-level data from 1994 to examine two of these implications: the impact of headquarter intensity and of productivity dispersion on the share of intrafirm imports. These data cover imports from 58 countries, which are classified into 51 manufacturing industries. Using capital intensity and R&D intensity as proxies for headquarter intensity, he finds that the share of intrafirm imports is higher in sectors with higher capital and R&D intensity and in sectors with more productivity dispersion. Both findings are in line with the theoretical predictions, and the former is in line with Antràs (2003).

Additional evidence on the positive correlation between headquarter intensity and the share of intrafirm imports is provided by Nunn and Trefler (2008), who use different—and much more detailed—data on U.S. trade.[158] These data cover more than 5,000 products, which they classify into 370 sectors, and imports from 210 countries in 2000 and 2005. Nunn and Trefler find that the share of intrafirm trade is larger in sectors with higher capital and skill intensity, which they interpret as sectors with higher headquarter intensity.[159] This positive correlation holds when controlling for exporting country characteristics. Similarly to Yeaple (2006), they find that the share of intrafirm imports is larger in sectors with higher productivity dispersion. Importantly, however, they construct five bins of headquarter intensity and estimate the impact of variation in headquarter intensity in each bin separately. The theory predicts that this effect should be nil in sectors with low headquarter intensity and positive in sectors with high headquarter intensity, which is what Nunn and Trefler find. Moreover, their results are similar whether they measure headquarter intensity with capital intensity or with skill intensity.[160]

Our theoretical discussion assumed that a firm needs only one type of component. In practice, however, many different intermediate inputs are needed to assemble a final product. As a result, a firm may choose different integration strategies for different intermediate inputs. In the case of a car, for example, the manufacturer may choose to produce the engine in-house in the home country, outsource the breaks to a local supplier in the home country, import the seats from an unaffiliated supplier in a foreign country, and import the windshields from its subsidiary in yet another country. In this example the firm engages in all four organizational forms. More generally, depending on the details of its technology, a firm may engage in any number of organizational forms. This point is clearly displayed in the Spanish data studied by Kohler and Smolka (2009). They use detailed firm-level data based on surveys of business strategies collected by the Sociedad Estatal de Participaciones Industriales. An attractive feature of this data set is that it reports how each firm acquires intermediate inputs: through outsourcing or integration, from home or abroad.

Table 6.2 reports the fraction of large firms (with more than 200 employees) that acquire intermediate inputs in each of the theoretical organizational modes. Of these firms, 34 percent produce their own inputs in Spain and 91 percent purchase inputs from unaffiliated Spanish suppliers, while 28 percent import inputs from their foreign subsidiaries and 66 percent import inputs from unaffiliated foreign firms. The sum of the numbers in the four cells of the table exceeds one because some firms engage in multiple sourcing strategies.[161] Among these firms only 1.5 percent produce intermediate inputs exclusively in-house in Spain, and only 17.7 percent exclusively outsource their inputs in Spain. Moreover, only 0.5 percent source inputs exclusively from foreign subsidiaries, and only 2.6 percent source exclusively from foreign unaffiliated parties. Taken together, these numbers imply that only 22.3 percent of the firms use a single organizational mode for the acquisition of their inputs; the rest use multiple organizational forms. Among the latter, 9.1 percent use all four organizational forms, and the largest fraction, 26.3 percent, use exclusively domestic and foreign outsourcing. Among the smaller firms, those with fewer than 200 employees, the majority, 56.3 percent,

Table 6.2.   Fraction of Spanish Firms in Each Organizational Mode, 2007

	Home	Offshore
Integration	0.34	0.28
Outsourcing	0.91	0.66

Source: Kohler and Smolka (2009, table 2).
Note: These data are for firms with more than 200 employees.

use exclusively domestic outsourcing, and 28.4 percent use exclusively domestic and foreign outsourcing (see Kohler and Smolka, 2009, table 1).

Assigning each firm to exactly one of the four organizational modes described in Table 6.2, on the basis of the organizational mode with the highest fixed cost among those practiced by the firm, Kohler and Smolka (2009) estimate productivity premia for every organizational form relative to domestic outsourcing. The results conform to the sorting pattern depicted in Figure 6.6; the productivity advantage is lowest for firms that outsource at home and highest for multinationals that import inputs from foreign subsidiaries, with Spanish firms that import intermediate inputs at arm's length having an intermediate productivity advantage. However, the productivity advantage of domestic integrated firms is not significantly different (in a statistical sense) from the productivity advantage of firms that import intermediates at arm's length. When the assignment of firms to the four bins is done in a nonexclusive way (a firm can belong to more than one bin), the ranking of the productivity premia is not as sharp. While it is still true that firms engaged in domestic outsourcing are less productive than other firms, the estimated productivity premia of the remaining three organizational forms are not significantly different from each other (in a statistical sense). To interpret this finding we need a richer model of sourcing, which is not yet available.

Support for the Antràs and Helpman (2004) model, albeit with a different ordering of fixed costs between integration and outsourcing, is provided by Defever and Toubal (2010) for French multinationals in 1999. These companies perceived the fixed cost of integration to be lower than the fixed cost of outsourcing. And with this ordering of the fixed costs, the theory predicts that among the offshoring firms the least productive should become multinationals and produce their intermediate inputs in foreign affiliates while the most productive should outsource their intermediate inputs. In this case intrafirm trade should take place among the low-productivity firms. As a result, a larger productivity dispersion should reduce the share of intrafirm trade.

In the French data, 21 percent of all transactions represent imports from affiliates only, 64 percent represent arm's-length imports only, and 15 percent represent imports of both types. In other words, as in the Spanish data, the division between outsourcing and integration is not as neat as suggested by the theory. Nonetheless, the productivity ordering is consistent with the theory: mean total factor productivity is 20 percent higher among the firms that import at arm's length than among those that import from affiliates (see Defever and Toubal, 2010, table 1). Moreover, the share of intrafirm imports is lower in sectors with more productivity dispersion.

It remains to consider the role of the *size* of contractual frictions, that is, the degree to which it is difficult to specify a detailed contract or to enforce one. In the previous discussion we assumed that the supply of inputs is not contractible; that is, no meaningful contract can be stipulated between the buyer and seller. Nevertheless, the degree of contractibility can vary across inputs. It can, for example, be different for components than for headquarter services. Antràs and Helpman (2008) extend the theory to allow for this type of variation. They show that in this case what matters is not so much the relative importance of headquarter services, but rather the relative importance of the *noncontractible* part of headquarter services. Namely, one should examine the fraction of noncontractible headquarter services times the headquarter services intensity of the production process relative to the fraction of noncontractible components times the components intensity of the production process. Moreover, in low headquarter-intensity sectors, where outsourcing dominates integration, the degree of contractibility should not affect the share of intrafirm imports. Nunn and Trefler (2008) find support for these predictions in the U.S. data.

The focus on firm-level trade provides important new insights on the international organization of production and the sourcing patterns of business firms. In addition, it sheds new light on the sectoral structure of trade, which goes far beyond the Ricardo, Heckscher-Ohlin, or

Helpman-Krugman models of trade. As the complexity of international patterns of specialization has increased over time, so has the theory of international trade and investment and the sophistication of empirical work on trade flows and activities of multinational corporations. As of now, the topics reviewed in this chapter are still among the most active research areas in international economics.

7

Epilogue

Aggregate measures of international engagement, such as trade volumes or stocks of FDI, do not fully reflect the extent of international interdependence. Over time, changes in these volumes were often driven by economic, technological, and political forces that also changed the nature of trade and investment flows around the world, thereby influencing the forms and degrees to which countries are tied in with each other. These developments also led to more complex interconnections across countries and business firms. As a result, the study of international economic activity had to be refocused time and again in order to appreciate and better understand the evolving channels through which countries influence each other's economies.

To help form such an understanding, this book provides an overview of what can be learned from the scholarly literature of the last two centuries. This literature is large and varied, consisting of theoretical, empirical, and historical studies, which provide a rich and fascinating account of the functioning of the global economy. Many of these studies are technical in nature, however, using mathematical models and statistical techniques, as a result of which they are accessible only to experts who have spent years of training in graduate schools. Yet the important insights from this literature can be explained in plain English, as demonstrated by the chapters of this book. Naturally, these explanations lack many, and sometimes valuable, details. But they remain true to the original findings and they cover the major themes from this literature.

Features of trade flows can be studied at the sectoral level, as was originally envisaged by the pioneers of this field, David Ricardo, Eli Heckscher, and Bertil Ohlin, or at the firm level, as was done more recently. Each of these approaches is suitable for addressing different issues. Indeed, the evolution of the entire field was driven by attempts to understand important characteristics of the world economy that either changed over time or surfaced as a result of new evidence. The chapters of this book were organized with this historical progression in mind, emphasizing the response of the profession to new evidence and changing circumstances. In the course of these developments, for example, monopolistic competition was introduced into trade theory and its empirical applications, and firm heterogeneity was added in order to address new issues. Similarly, the traditional approach to the organization of production—in which boundaries of business firms are not well defined—was replaced by more sophisticated views, which include decisions to offshore and outsource parts of the value chain. We now have a rich theory and a large body of evidence that identify many channels of interdependence across national economies, as well as a much more sophisticated and nuanced view of the structure of trade and FDI in the global economy.

While the story line of this book has covered a lot of ground, there are a number of themes with which it has not dealt. Two of these themes have received much attention in recent studies, while others have not. Let me elaborate on each of them.

One theme concerns the role of multiproduct firms. Such firms were not discussed in the previous chapters; there every firm was treated as a seller of a single product or a single brand of a differentiated product. It is, however, well known that many firms manufacture multiple products, and these firms are big and important. According to the classification of Bernard, Redding and Schott (2010a, table 1), in 1997, 39 percent of U.S. manufacturing firms supplied multiple products and these firms accounted for 87 percent of shipments. That is, while multiproduct firms formed a large minority of the population of firms, they controlled a large majority of production. Moreover, such firms feature prominently in international trade. Bernard, Jensen, Redding and Schott (2007, table 4) report that, in 2000, single-product exporters in U.S. manufacturing accounted for 42.2 percent of U.S. exporting firms in this industry, while firms that exported at least five products accounted for 25.9 percent of exporters. On the other hand, the single-product firms accounted for 0.4 percent of the value of exports, while the multiproduct firms with at least five products accounted for 98 percent of this value. In other words, although the multiproduct exporters with at least five products constituted a large minority of firms, they overwhelmingly dominated U.S. exports.

In view of this evidence, one may wonder how much potential for understanding global trade flows is lost in the simpler view of the world, which disregards multiproduct firms. The answer to this question is not clear. On the one hand, current theoretical studies of trade with multi-product firms emphasize a particular extensive margin (i.e., the number of products per firm), which responds to trade and trade liberalization.[162] Indeed, exporters differ from nonexporters not only in productivity and size; they also manufacture more products and vary the number of exported products across countries. For these reasons it makes sense to explore the role of multiproduct firms in international trade. On the other hand, the empirical studies, such as Bernard, Redding, and Schott (2010b) and Arkolakis and Muendler (2008), have not yet shown convincingly that we need to change in important ways our view of trade due to the existence of multiproduct firms. However, the verdict on this line of research is not final, and more detailed studies that examine multinational corporations and economic growth may lead to different conclusions.

A second theme concerns the quality of traded products, which was very briefly touched on in Chapter 4. Measurement issues arise concerning the quality of products, and particularly so when studying trade across a large number of countries, because data on quality is not readily available. As a result, scholars try to infer quality indirectly from observations of other economic variables. Under the circumstances the accumulated evidence paints an uncertain picture of the role of quality in foreign trade.

One approach treats unit values of exports, which represent price indexes of export baskets, as measures of quality.[163] According to this view, higher unit values reflect higher-quality products. Since richer countries export goods with higher unit values, this is interpreted to mean that a country's income per capita is positively correlated with the quality of its exports.[164] Also, using this measure, researchers have found that a country's higher-quality exports are disproportionately directed to higher-income countries (see Hallak, 2006).

The problem is, however, that unit values are an imprecise measure of quality at best, because they differ across countries for reasons besides quality. For example, if in addition to vertical product differentiation (that is, differentiation by quality) there is horizontal product differentiation of the type discussed in Chapters 4 through 6, then unit values of exports can differ across countries when they export a different number of brands, even when the quality of their exports is the same. Under these circumstances countries with more diversified exports have lower unit values. Hallak and Schott (2010) develop a methodology to purge this element from the sectoral data in order to obtain a more reliable measure of the quality of exports, and they show that this correction has significant implications for the quality of exports to the United States from 43 countries between 1989 and 2003.[165] They still find in the cross-section that the quality of exports was positively correlated with the exporter's income per capita, but they also find that during those years the quality levels of different countries' exports converged while their incomes per capita did not.

Hallak and Schott also find that country rankings by export quality have changed significantly over time (see Hallak and Schott, 2010, table IV). Switzerland had the highest quality of exports in 1989 and it moved down to rank 4 in 2003, while Ireland moved up from rank 11 to rank 1. Singapore and Malaysia were big winners; the former moved up from rank 27 to rank 2, while the latter moved up from rank 42 to 7. On the other side, Australia and New Zealand moved down the quality ladder, while China remained close to its original position (it moved from rank 35 to 37). All these findings are interesting, but they have built-in measurement errors whose extent is as yet unknown.

Export prices from firm-level data have also been used to study trade patterns in products of varying quality, accounting for firm heterogeneity within industries.[166] Unfortunately, the discomfort with the use of price as a measure of quality at the sectoral level applies to this research too. Verhoogen (2008) is an exception. Instead of price, he uses a certification standard as a measure of quality to investigate quality upgrading by Mexican firms of their exports to the United States after an exchange rate shock. But even in this study, the measure of quality is coarse.

Another issue concerns methodology. While most studies use constant-elasticity-of-substitution functions to assess horizontal and vertical product differentiation, Khandelwal (2009) and Verhoogen (2008) use variants of a logit model. Sheu (2010) shows, however, that estimates of gains from product variety are sensitive to the estimation method. She uses detailed data on imports of printers to India, which include key characteristics of these products, such as speed. From these data she estimates welfare gains from trade using Feenstra's (1994) methodology for two versions of a constant-elasticity-of-substitution demand function, and a random-coefficient discrete-choice model à la Berry, Levinsohn, and Pakes (1995). And she shows how the resulting estimates vary with the methodology. While Sheu uses a particular product to illustrate the dependence of the estimates on the methodology—and the results may be different for other products—her findings sound a cautionary note for the interpretation of the evidence.

Despite these difficulties, I believe that the potential gains from better understanding trade in varying-quality products are substantial. One area in which quality may prove to be particularly important is the analysis of economic growth and development, in which the study of multiproduct firms may also be important. The reason for this assessment is that economic growth is driven by the accumulation of human capital, physical capital, and total factor productivity growth. The last is of particular importance, as has been emphasized by the growth literature of the last two and a half decades.[167] According to this view, TFP can rise as a result of innovation, which either reduces costs, expands the array of final and intermediate goods, or raises the quality of inputs and consumer products. Additional spurs include the development of general-purpose technologies and institutions, where the latter serve as enablers of technological change. For current purposes, however, variety growth and quality upgrading are of particular interest, and each of these can feed long-run growth and development. Since international trade stimulates incentives to invent entirely new products and to upgrade the quality of existing products, it impacts growth and development through these channels. For this reason a better understanding of how trade influences the diversity and quality of products can lead to a better understanding of growth and development and thereby to more effective economic policies designed to raise standards of living.

While the growth literature provides an appreciation of these channels of influence, its insights rely on models from the 1990s.[168] In particular, these models do not account for various margins of adjustment to international trade that have been identified more recently, such as the extensive margin of trade and the quality of traded products.[169] If the extensive margin of trade proves to be important for growth, then multiproduct firms may also prove to be important, because they play an essential role in the determination of the range of traded products. And specialization along quality levels in industries with vertical product differentiation can significantly affect growth. The quality-ladder models of Grossman and Helpman (1991) and Aghion and Howitt (1992) speak to this issue in a rudimentary way, while recent advances in international trade with varying-quality products can provide new insights on the workings of this mechanism, significantly beyond the simple versions of the quality-ladder models.

Moreover, in a growth context it is possible to allow the productivity of a business firm to change as a result of technological upgrading. Under these circumstances the distribution of firm productivity is endogenous and changes over time. The incentives of firms with different productivity levels to upgrade their technologies depends, however, on foreign trade, which introduces an additional link between trade and productivity growth.[170] In short, by integrating the new view of international trade into a modern growth-and-development framework, we can gain an improved understanding of how standards of living can be raised in a globalized world.

Notes

1. Both McCormick (2001, chapter 4) and Ward-Perkins (2005) refer to archaeological evidence on pottery finds as measures of living standards and trade. For example, McCormick notes: "From the third century African goods increasingly prevail among detectible wares arriving at Ostia and Rome. They displaced, most notably, the Spanish oil imports whose 53 million (estimated) broken containers still form a 'mountain' along the Tiber" (p. 100). This "mountain" is also discussed by Ward-Perkins.

2. The regions are western Europe, eastern Europe, the Islamic world, Sub-Saharan Africa, Central Asia, South Asia, Southeast Asia, and East Asia.

3. O'Rourke and Williamson (1999) provide a comprehensive treatment of the process of "globalization" in the late nineteenth and early twentieth centuries.

4. I am grateful to Kevin O'Rourke for providing the data and permitting their use for the construction of this figure.

5. I am grateful to Alan Taylor for providing the data and permitting their use for the construction of this figure.

6. Pomeranz (2000) also emphasizes the role of coal.

7. The British Glorious Revolution of 1688 is considered the prime example of such changes in political institutions. According to North and Weingast (1989), it also greatly improved British finances, which played a major role in subsequent economic developments.

8. In this case the monarch also became a sequential defaulter on debts, thus hurting Spanish economic development.

9. This statement needs to be qualified, because trade in factor services introduces absolute advantage considerations into the determinants of international trade flows; see Jones (1980).

10. This argument assumes that labor can be employed either in the production of cloth or in the production of wine, and that no other employment opportunities exist.

11. The role of demand conditions in determining relative prices was first discussed in 1848 by Mill (1909) in his chapter "On International Values."

12. Although Ricardo does not discuss this explicitly, his example has been interpreted as representing differences in the technological capabilities of England and Portugal rather than differences in the skill composition of their workers. This interpretation is consistent with Ricardo's observation that it would be efficient to move all English workers to Portugal if this were possible. Implicit in this statement is the assumption that English workers residing in Portugal can produce quantities equal to those of Portuguese workers, because by residing in Portugal they gain access to Portuguese technology.

13. McKenzie (1953–1954) contains a discussion of Ricardian systems with intermediate inputs.

14. This argument assumes that there are no transport costs, tariffs, or other impediments to trade, and that there is competition in all markets that leads to price-taking behavior by everyone. I shall discuss deviation from this extreme form of competition in Chapter 4.

15. I assume in this discussion that wine is a homogeneous product (i.e., different manufacturers of wine in either Portugal or France offer bottles of wine that are perfect substitutes for each other). This is obviously not true about wine, and neither is it true about many other products, such as garments, drugs, or cars. I will take up product differentiation and brand proliferation in Chapter 4.

16. I assume, as is common in this type of analysis, that every country has balanced trade. Deviations from trade balance are important in practice, but typically they have minor effects on the direction of trade.

17. Because of budget constraints it is not possible for the demand for labor to exceed the supply in both countries, and it also is impossible for the demand to fall short of the supply in both countries.

18. Dornbusch, Fischer, and Samuelson (1977) include many products, each one represented by a point on a line interval. This representation is convenient for technical reasons but does not affect the economic insights. They also use constant expenditure shares to simplify demand so that Ricardo's argument about supply is made more transparent. Wilson (1980) provides a generalization. Earlier important contributions to this literature include Graham (1948) and McKenzie (1954).

19. A decline in the price of exportables relative to the price of importables is called a deterioration in the terms of trade.

20. Sometimes a country stores part of the payment it receives for its exports in the form of foreign assets. But if these foreign assets are never used to pay for goods and services, they obviously do not contribute to the country's well-being. It therefore follows that even if such export proceeds are not used immediately to pay for imports, they eventually will be. The Mercantilistic view from the sixteenth and seventeenth centuries that the accumulation of gold or silver (via an excess of exports over imports) contributes directly to a nation's prosperity has been dispelled by modern scholars.

21. This is known as the "melting iceberg" formulation of transport costs, which was originally introduced by Samuelson (1954). (The analogy is to an iceberg that melts partly on the way when shipped from its origin to a faraway destination.) Helpman (1976) develops an international trade model in which transport technology is treated the same way as production technology, and Matsuyama (2007) develops a model in the spirit of Dornbusch, Fischer, and Samuelson (1977) in which the technology for supplying the foreign market differs from the technology for supplying the domestic market.

22. A number of studies published in the 1950s and 1960s examined the relationship between relative costs and relative exports to third markets in order to test Ricardo's theory (see McDougall, 1951, 1952; and Stern, 1962). As it happens, however, the theory does not predict a clear relationship between these variables in a multicountry world. For this reason the findings of these studies, while interesting, are of limited value as tests of the theory.

23. More precisely, they assume that labor productivity follows a Fréchet (or Type II extreme value) distribution.

24. Eaton and Kortum (2002) do not describe in detail the general equilibrium structure of their model. Instead, they only develop equations that

are needed for predicting trade flows across country pairs. Alvarez and Lucas (2007) develop the full general equilibrium implications of the Eaton-Kortum model.

25. Heckscher's original article was published in 1919 in *Economisk Tidskrift* 21: 497–512, a Swedish journal of economics. It was first translated in abridged form into English in 1949. An updated translation of the entire article, titled "The Effect of Foreign Trade on the Distribution of Income," appears in Flam and Flanders (1991). Ohlin's original contribution was published in Swedish in 1924 as a Ph.D. dissertation, submitted to what is now the University of Stockholm. A complete translation of the dissertation, titled "The Theory of Trade," also appears in Flam and Flanders (1991). An expanded version of the dissertation was published as a book in 1933 under the title *Interregional and International Trade*; see Ohlin (1933).

26. After studying with Eli Heckscher, Ohlin proceeded to write a dissertation with Gustav Cassel, who was Heckscher's intellectual rival. Ohlin's bonding with Cassel caused tensions between him and Heckscher. See Flam and Flanders (1991).

27. A technology exhibits economies of scale if a proportional expansion of all inputs raises output more than proportionately. And a technology exhibits diseconomies of scale if a proportional expansion of all inputs raises output less than proportionately. A technology exhibits neither economies of scale nor diseconomies of scale if a proportional expansion of all inputs raises output by the same factor of proportionality. Heckscher, and particularly Ohlin, discuss economies of scale as an independent source of comparative costs. I will examine the role of economies of scale in Chapter 4.

28. An almost identical statement about the role of relative scarcity (i.e., the relative prices of factors of production) is made by Ohlin: "The conclusion therefore is that the cause of interregional trade lies in a difference in the relative scarcity of productive factors, which in each region manifests itself in lower absolute prices of some factors and goods and higher prices of other factors and goods relative to those 'abroad.' It is this difference in the absolute costs of production and prices that is the immediate cause of trade and that leads to each region's specializing in the output of those goods that it can produce more cheaply than others" (Ohlin, 1924, p. 89 in Flam and Flanders, 1991).

29. Ohlin did not consider factor price equalization to be a likely outcome, however. See further discussion on the effects of trade on factor prices later in this chapter and in the next chapter.

30. Ford (1982) pointed out that whenever the relative prices of capital and labor differ across countries, there are circumstances (e.g., when the elasticity of substitution between labor and capital is the same in all industries) in which the Heckscher-Ohlin model acquires a key property of the Ricardian model: the ranking of sectoral relative labor requirements coincides with the ranking of relative costs. Under these circumstances the relative labor requirements are not driven by geographic or "natural" characteristics, as in Ricardo's world, but rather by variation across sectors in capital use per unit output.

31. The ex-ante and ex-post predictions may not coincide if there is factor-intensity reversal, meaning that the ordering of sectors by factor intensity is sensitive to factor prices. In these circumstances the ordering of sectors by factor intensity given one set of factor prices differs from the ordering of sectors by factor intensity given a different set of factor prices. See Chipman (1966) for a review of the literature on this subject.

32. Simple derivations of this important result are available in Dixit and Norman (1980, chapter 4) and Helpman and Krugman (1985, chapter 1).

33. Like many economic models, this one focuses on a particular issue and has counterfactual implications in other dimensions. When this is the case, the big question is how robust the model's predictions concerning the issue on which it focuses are. This is discussed in more detail later in this chapter.

34. This requires constructing the data in a way that ensures that the number of sectors are the same as the number of factors of production and that the resulting input requirements per unit output satisfy a technical condition of independence across sectors. Leamer (1984) did indeed construct his data in this fashion.

35. I use net exports as the variable of interest because at the common levels of aggregation of sectoral data sets countries import and export products within sectors (this is known as "intra-industry trade"), yet the theory predicts trade in one direction only. This issue will be discussed in more detail in Chapter 4. For now note that if a country exports more than it imports, its net exports are positive, and if a country exports less than it imports, its net exports are negative.

36. Leamer's (1984) data cover sixty countries and eleven factors of production: capital; three types of labor, differentiated by skill levels; four types of land, differentiated by climatic qualities; coal; minerals; and oil. It also covers eleven sectors, ten of which are listed in the table. The eleventh sector is defined as the remaining part of gross national product (GNP).

37. We shall not be concerned with the size of these coefficients, which are estimated with different degrees of precision, but rather with their signs only (i.e., whether they are positive or negative).

38. Leamer (1984) finds that the linear relationship is a good approximation in all the sectors except machinery and chemicals, where the data point to possible nonlinearities.

39. In Hunter (1991), identical preferences are assumed to prevail in all countries, except that budget shares depend on per capita income (i.e., preferences are not homothetic). A linear expenditure system is estimated for 34 countries over 11 commodity aggregates. A counterfactual exercise is conducted to estimate the volume of trade caused by deviations from homotheticity of preferences. The results suggest that nonhomothetic preferences may account for as much as one-quarter of interindustry trade flows.

40. Following Leamer's insight, a large number of studies examined linear relationships between inputs and outputs. For examples, see Harrigan (1995) and Reeve (2006).

41. The constancy of sectoral factor-intensity levels is often ensured by assuming that commodity prices do not change, and as a result neither do factor prices.

42. The Rybczynski Theorem, the Heckscher-Ohlin Theorem, and many other results for the case of two sectors and two factors of production are most elegantly derived in Jones (1965).

43. Fitzgerald and Hallak (2004) show that customary estimates of Rybczynski coefficients are biased because they do not account for productivity differences across countries. This bias also explains the common finding that capital has a positive effect on the output levels of most manufacturing industries.

44. The assumption of factor price equalization is strong; it requires the composition of factor endowments not to differ across countries too much. And, as will be explained later, it has particularly strong implications for factor content analysis.

45. These predictions do not depend on the number of primary inputs or the number of sectors, as long as there is factor price equalization. However, the latter is more likely when there are more goods than factors.

46. Instead of consumption, we should use domestic absorption, which consists of consumption, investment, and government spending. For clarity of the exposition, however, I will refer to consumption.

47. As it turns out, other relationships in the data are inconsistent with the United States being capital-rich; see Brecher and Choudhri (1982) and the following discussion of the empirical tests of the Vanek equations.

48. Trefler (1993) estimates country-level factor-biased technology differences in a model that assumes that the modified Vanek equations hold exactly. He shows that the resulting measures of labor productivity are highly correlated with wages and the resulting measures of capital productivity are correlated with capital costs.

49. Davis, Weinstein, Bradford, and Shimpo (1997) find that differences in input-output coefficients are not needed to explain the factor content of trade across Japanese regions. This is consistent with the view that factor prices are more similar across regions of a country than across countries.

50. These laws were repealed in 1846, when Britain adopted a free trade policy.

51. This statement assumes that individuals have no direct preferences about the mechanism that allocates goods in the economy, only about the allocation itself. Naturally, this is unlikely to be the case, because people may be less happy in a command economy than in an economy with free choice.

52. The implicit assumption in this argument is that the marginal rate of transformation between pasta and cheese does not depend on the direction of the transformation (i.e., on whether we increase the production of pasta or the production of cheese). This is a common assumption in economic models, but it is not essential for the gains-from-trade argument.

53. In this illustration, resources shift costlessly from one sector to another, which means that it disregards possible costs of adjustment to trade opening. These costs can take the form of temporarily idle inputs or of actual costs of dislocation, such as moving expenses.

54. Since every individual owns an identical combination of resources, each one has the same income and therefore faces the same budget constraint.

Under the circumstances, every individual chooses the same consumption basket, because they all have identical preferences.

55. See Dixit and Norman (1980) for an elegant proof.

56. Here is the place to invoke the trade-balance constraint, as is normally done in the theory of international trade.

57. These conversion rates are not constant if the country's trade flows are big enough to impact international prices. This possibility does not affect the argument in the text, however.

58. Irwin's low estimate is 4.2 percent of GNP and his high estimate is 5.5 percent.

59. See Bernhofen and Brown (2005).

60. The difference between these two output measures is positive in neo-classical economies.

61. I am grateful to John Brown for providing the data for this figure.

62. This result stems from the fact that in the trading equilibrium the purchasing power of a worker's wage is at least as high in terms of every good as it is in autarky. The reason is that it is the same in terms of goods that the country manufactures in the trade equilibrium, but higher in terms of the imported products that are cheaper in the foreign countries.

63. If the price of wine is more than 50 percent higher than the price of cloth, both England and Portugal want to export wine, and if it is less than 35 percent higher than the price of cloth, then both England and Portugal want to import wine. Neither of these outcomes is feasible. For prices of wine that are between 35 percent and 50 percent higher than the price of cloth, England wants to import wine while Portugal wants to export it. Moreover, under standard assumptions about preferences there exists a price in between at which English imports of wine just equal Portuguese exports.

64. Here is the argument. In a competitive economy with constant returns to scale, the price of a product equals its unit cost. Therefore, when the price of a product rises, there has to be a hike in the price of at least one input to ensure an equal rise in the product's unit cost. But other unit costs do not change because the other prices do not change. Therefore, if some factor rewards increase, there have to be other factor rewards that decline. This establishes that at least one factor reward has to decline. If at least one factor reward declines and the unit cost of the product whose

price has increased rises proportionately to the price hike, there has to be an input price that rises proportionately more than the product price. Why? Because the weighted average of all factor reward increases has to equal the rise in the product price, and therefore the decline in a factor reward has to be compensated for by a more than proportional increase in another factor reward.

65. A more general analysis of this issue is provided in Ohyama (1972).

66. In a large country the redistribution scheme affects international prices. But this does not change the nature of the argument, as long as the price ratio considered in the trading equilibrium is the price ratio that results in the presence of the redistribution scheme. The point is that the argument in the text applies to every conceivable price structure.

67. To see why, note that aggregate private net income equals in this economy GDP minus lump-sum taxes plus lump-sum subsidies. From the choice of redistribution scheme, this net private income equals the value of autarky consumption, evaluated with the international prices. But autarky consumption equals autarky production. As a result, net private income equals the value of autarky production, evaluated with the international prices. This implies that the government's net tax collection (taxes minus subsidies) equals GDP minus what the country's GDP would be if it were to produce in the trading equilibrium the autarky output levels. Since competition in a neoclassical economy ensures the highest GDP at the prevailing prices, this difference is positive, and therefore the government has a budget surplus. See Dixit and Norman (1980) for an alternative (yet related) argument that shows lump-sum taxes and subsidies exist that ensure gains from trade for all.

68. I thank Peter Klenow for providing the data for this figure. Additional features of trade that require thinking beyond traditional comparative advantage will be discussed later in the chapter.

69. Krugman (1979) and Lancaster (1979, chapter 10) developed the first formal one-sector models of trade in a differentiated product. Although their models differ in various details, both are designed to show how trade in different brands of the same product arises within an industry. Lancaster (1980), Dixit and Norman (1980, chapter 9), and Helpman (1981) integrated product differentiation with factor proportions, showing how intra-industry and intersectoral trade can coexist. Helpman and

Krugman (1985) developed a comprehensive treatment of what became known as the "new trade theory." All these studies build on the seminal work of Chamberlin (1933).

70. Although in principle a technology can exhibit economies of scale for some input combinations and diminishing returns for other input combinations, such complications are usually assumed away.

71. For simplicity, we disregard his use of tools.

72. Helpman and Krugman (1985, chapter 3) provide a detailed discussion of these issues and place Graham's argument in a broader context. They also discuss external economies that are not country specific (i.e., cases in which a firm's productivity depends on the world's output of the industry rather than on the domestic output). In the latter case, as Viner argued, Graham's conjecture does not hold.

73. It cannot charge a price that exceeds its average cost because another firm could then undercut this price and make positive profits.

74. Unlike the traditional Ricardian world, here the possibility exists that a country might not gain from trade. Grossman and Rossi-Hansberg (2010) show, however, that if preferences exhibit a constant elasticity of substitution across all products, then not only is the pattern of specialization unique, but every country gains from trade.

75. Caves, Christensen, and Swanson (1981) estimate large economies of scale (i.e., declining average cost) in U.S. railroads for the period between 1955 and 1974, while Christensen and Greene (1976) find large economies of scale in U.S. electric power generation in 1955, which peter out in the 1970s.

76. These sectors' scale economies are larger, however, than the economies of scale in the natural resource industries mentioned, except for forestry. Estimates of the degree of scale economies in other sectors—such as basic chemicals, pulp and paper, glass products, and tobacco—are not sharp enough to classify their economies of scale.

77. Porter (1990) provides many such examples, although he emphasizes that economies of agglomeration play a key role in the formation of the competitive advantage of nations.

78. Helpman and Krugman (1985) also discuss various forms of oligopolistic competition that are suitable for industries with limited product differentiation. These market structures are less important for the main story of this book, however.

79. In addition to scale economies related to fixed costs, output volume may also give rise to scale economies. That is, variable unit costs of manufacturing may decline with the output level.

80. See http://www.fda.gov/buyonlineguide/generics_q&a.htm, accessed on March 10, 2009.

81. The empirical definition of a variety in this study is a product imported from a particular country. For example, in 1988 there were 12,822 product categories, each one imported from an average of 12.2 countries, yielding in total 156,669 brands. See Broda and Weinstein (2006, table 1).

82. The variety-adjusted price index measures the cost of a unit of imports, where this unit is defined in terms of a contribution to welfare, taking into account not only import prices but also the range of imported varieties.

83. Unlike the factor proportions approach with homogeneous products, the Ricardian approach with homogeneous products is consistent with the gravity equation.

84. See also Helpman and Krugman (1985).

85. The factor of proportionality in this case equals 2 divided by the world's GDP level, which is the same for every country pair. A similar calculation applies to the Ricardian model of Dornbusch, Fischer, and Samuelson (1977) or Eaton and Kortum (2002), because in these cases, too, every country produces distinct products.

86. This hypothesis about factor proportions versus intra-industry specialization in the trade between rich countries was raised by Hummels and Levinsohn (1995), who then argued that it is rejected by the data. But Debaere (2005) shows that this rejection is driven by an inappropriate specification of their trade equation, in which the trade volume is estimated in level form rather than as a fraction of GDP. Moreover, Evenett and Keller (2002) show that similarity in income levels provides a better explanation of bilateral trade flows the larger the share of intra-industry trade is between the pair of trading countries. In other words, the forces of gravity are more pronounced the more important trade is in differentiated products, as suggested by the theory.

87. Although closer alignment of GDP per capita can be driven by factors other than closer similarity in capital-labor ratios, the correlation between the two measures of similarity is very high in the data, and GDP per capita is more accurately measured than the capital-labor ratio.

88. Hanson and Xiang (2004) extend Krugman's model to justify these claims.

89. See Fajgelbaum, Grossman, and Helpman (2009).

90. I am grateful to John Romalis for providing the data for this figure.

91. His study represents part of a broader trend to investigate the roles of institutions in shaping economic activity.

92. Grossman and Hart (1986) and Hart and Moore (1990) pioneered the analysis of economic relations in environments with incomplete contracts. We will discuss their approach in Chapter 6.

93. Levchenko (2007) also finds support for the impact of differences across countries in the quality of legal systems on trade flows, although he uses a measure of sectoral complexity instead of contractual intensity in his estimation. Costinot (2009) too studies the role of sectoral complexity on trade flows, except that he backs out differences in the quality of legal systems from estimates of trade flows. His revealed measure of institutional quality is highly correlated with a measure called "The Rule of Law" that is also used by Nunn (2007); see Costinot (2009, figure 4).

94. See Baldwin and Gu (2003) for Canada; Clerides, Lach, and Tybout (1998) for Colombia, Mexico, and Morocco; Bernard, Eaton, Jensen, and Kortum (2003) and Eaton, Kortum, and Kramarz (2004) for France; Delgado, Fariñas, and Ruano (2002) for Spain; and Aw, Chung, and Roberts (2000) for Taiwan.

95. See Roberts and Tybout (1997) for Colombia and Bernard and Jensen (2004) for the United States.

96. See Bernard, Jensen, Redding, and Schott (2007, table 2).

97. See Bernard, Jensen, Redding, and Schott (2007, table 3).

98. See Bernard, Jensen, Redding, and Schott (2007, table 2).

99. Bernard, Eaton, Jensen, and Kortum (2003) developed an alternative model for explaining the same findings. Yet Melitz's framework has become the profession's standard.

100. For now I do not consider the option of foreign direct investment, which is discussed in Chapter 6.

101. The former means, in particular, that the composition of inputs in activities that generate variable costs, such as manufacturing, is the same as in activities that generate fixed costs, such as research and development (R&D).

102. See Anderson and van Wincoop (2003) for a recent contribution to this literature.

103. In Helpman, Melitz, and Rubinstein's sample of 158 countries, roughly half the bilateral observations consist of zero trade.

104. The two models compared by Balistreri, Hillberry, and Rutherford have the same parameters and the same average productivity of firms in the manufacturing sector, which were estimated or calibrated with data. In the "standard" model the average productivity of firms does not change with trade liberalization, while in the model with heterogeneous firms it does.

105. Reductions of markups (the gap between the price of a product and its marginal cost of production) can also be a source of gains from trade or trade liberalization. On this mechanism see Melitz and Ottaviano (2008) and Feenstra and Weinstein (2010).

106. Feenstra (2009) provides a clear explanation of this analytical result, showing that it very much depends on the assumption in the Demidova, Klenow, and Rodríguez-Clare analysis that the elasticity of substitution is constant across varieties. With a varying elasticity of substitution there is no perfect offset of foreign and home entry into the domestic market.

107. See the European Commission, http://ec.europa.eu/social/main.jsp ?catId=101&langId=en, accessed on September 25, 2009.

108. See the European Parliament, http://www.europarl.europa.eu/summits/ lis1_en.htm, accessed on September 25, 2009.

109. Table 5.4 reports these indexes for a small sample of countries; the World Bank website provides indexes for over 100 countries.

110. See the textbook treatment in Pissarides (2000). The literature on trade and labor market frictions includes studies of minimum wages, such as Brecher (1974); implicit contracts, such as Matusz (1986); and efficiency wages, such as Copeland (1989).

111. See Pissarides (2000) for the former and Davidson, Martin, and Matusz (1999) for the latter.

112. More recently, search and matching have been integrated into the analysis of business cycles; see Shimer (2005).

113. See http://www.bls.gov/news.release/jolts.htm and http://www.bls.gov/ news.release/empsit.t08.htm, accessed on September 29, 2009.

114. Although most of this research considers dynamic situations with flows in and out of employment that lead to unemployment in the long run,

I will abstract from dynamics and simplify the analysis by considering static environments, as has been done so far in this book. For this purpose it is useful to think about a matching process that leads to a number of matches that is smaller than both the number of vacancies and the number of individuals searching for work. Under these circumstances, not all vacancies are filled and not all workers find employment.

115. I disregard policies, such as unemployment insurance and severance pay. See, however, the discussion in Helpman and Itskhoki (2010).

116. The cost of hiring a worker equals the vacancy cost divided by the probability of filling a vacancy, and this measure, which plays a key role in the following analysis, can be different in the homogeneous and the differentiated sectors.

117. See http://www.bls.gov/cps/cpsaat26.pdf, accessed on September 29, 2009.

118. In the homogeneous sector, the firm and each worker equally share the surplus from their relationship. In the differentiated-product sector, wage bargaining is multilateral, in the form proposed by Stole and Zwiebel (1996a,b).

119. This result also implies that, labor market frictions notwithstanding, both countries gain from trade.

120. These figures depict patterns reported in Helpman and Itskhoki (2010), which were derived from numerical simulations in which there are no labor market frictions in the homogeneous-product sector.

121. This type of wage inequality is often referred to as "residual" or "within group" wage inequality; see Lemieux (2006) and Autor, Katz, and Kearney (2008) for evidence.

122. See Helpman (2004, chapter 6) for a review of the evidence and alternative explanations. See also the discussion on rising inequality in Goldberg and Pavcnik (2007).

123. As of now, quantitative evidence to form a judgment on this issue is lacking.

124. See Helpman, Itskhoki, and Redding (2010b) for this result and the following discussion.

125. This figure is based on the simulations reported in Helpman, Itskhoki, and Redding (2010b).

126. See Rajan and Wulf (2006) for evidence on the flattening of the hierarchical management structure.

127. For evidence, see Bardi and Tracey (1991) on transportation, Gardner (1991) on health care, Helper (1991) on automobiles, and Abraham and Taylor (1996) and Bartel, Lach, and Sicherman (2005) on other sectors.

128. In addition, Hummels, Ishii, and Yi (2001) and Yeats (2001) find that international trade in intermediate inputs grew faster than trade in final goods, and Yi (2003) develops a model with stages of production to explain this trend. Trade among affiliates of U.S. multinationals also grew at a fast pace, although somewhat slower than foreign outsourcing by U.S. firms; see Hanson, Mataloni, and Slaughter (2005). Finally, Alfaro and Charlton (2009) argue that vertical FDI is often misclassified as horizontal FDI when the analysis is done with commonly used aggregation levels of data sets. According to their calculations, with highly disaggregated data, the shares of vertical and horizontal FDI are very similar.

129. See UNCTAD (2008). The preceding peak of FDI inflows was in excess of $1.4 trillion in 2000, but FDI collapsed with the drop in the share prices of high-technology companies and fell to $560 billion in 2003; see UNCTAD (2004). Nevertheless, the 2000 peak was recovered in 2006, and FDI had climbed even higher by 2007; see UNCTAD (2008, table 2.1).

130. See UNCTAD (2008, table 2.1).

131. UNCTAD's World Investment Reports provide measures of the stock of FDI in addition to flows, which better reflect the involvement of multinationals in foreign countries. For example, in 2007 the FDI inward stock was $15.2 trillion while the FDI inflow was $1.8 trillion (see UNCTAD, 2008, table 1.4). But even the FDI stock does not measure properly the extent of control that multinationals have in foreign countries, because they often leverage their investments with loans from host-country financial institutions and these loans can be quite large relative to the parent firm's investment. Moreover, even corrections of FDI stocks for local financing would not correlate accurately with capital investment, sales, or the employment of subsidiaries of multinational companies.

132. Affiliated parties are the parent and subsidiaries of a multinational corporation.

133. These numbers are somewhat sensitive to definitions. In the statistics of the Bureau of Economic Analysis, an affiliate is defined as a foreign entity in which the parent firm holds at least a 10 percent ownership for exporters and 6 percent for importers. Under this definition many firms

are counted as multinational corporations. A stricter definition would count only majority-owned affiliates. According to Bernard, Jensen, Redding, and Schott (2010b), who use data on majority-owned multinational corporations, intrafirm imports amounted to only 46 percent of U.S. imports in 2000. This share varied greatly across foreign exporters: about 3.5 percent for imports from Pakistan, 18 percent for imports from China, 26.6 percent for imports from Russia, close to 65 percent for imports from Germany, and 97 percent for imports from New Caledonia.

134. It can impact foreign trade indirectly because the home supplier of engines may need to import steel or other inputs to fulfill the car manufacturer's order.

135. Indeed, Zhu and Trefler (2005) show that a similar result obtains when the less-developed country trades with the developed country and no FDI flows across their borders, but when the less-developed country catches up technologically to the developed country.

136. Both Helpman (1984b) and Markusen (1984) *assume* that when a firm finds it profitable to build a plant in a foreign country it also finds it profitable to retain control of the subsidiary. Ethier (1986) constructs a model in which the control decision is explicitly analyzed. I will come back to the internalization decision in section 6.5.

137. See Grossman, Helpman, and Szeidl (2006) and Ekholm, Forslid, and Markusen (2007) for a discussion of this type of FDI.

138. While Dunning's eclectic approach may not be structured enough for clear theoretical predictions, it fed a large empirical literature. Much of this literature is reviewed in Caves (2007). Of particular interest is that these studies have identified sectoral characteristics that correlated with FDI.

139. It is best to think about this firm as a supplier of a brand of a differentiated product, although the same type of reasoning has been applied to homogeneous goods. For the latter, see Markusen (1984).

140. In the figure, the profit curves are linear, although typically they will have some curvature. The important feature is that both curves are rising with market size, while their curvature is not important for the following arguments.

141. It was also argued at the time that Japanese car manufacturers engage in preemptive FDI, in anticipation of higher rates of protection in the United States. See the discussion in Grossman and Helpman (1996).

142. The role of market size is emphasized in Carr, Markusen, and Maskus (2001).

143. See the discussion of the Melitz model in the previous chapter.

144. In some of these studies the pecking order is reported for labor productivity, in others for TFP. Tomiura (2007) reports both.

145. Helpman, Melitz, and Yeaple (2004) report similar estimates for a larger sample of 38 destination countries.

146. The shape parameter of a Pareto distribution represents a measure of dispersion, with larger values representing less dispersion.

147. Recall that the factor content predictions are that a country exports the factor content of every input with which it is well endowed relative to the world and imports the factor content of every input with which it is poorly endowed relative to the world. The Vanek (1968) equations provide a precise formulation of these relationships.

148. More precisely, Yeaple (2003b) regresses exports divided by exports plus subsidiary sales on the variables that are affiliated with horizontal and vertical FDI.

149. In Malaysia, exports back to the United States were 39 percent and exports to third countries were 28 percent of total sales of U.S. subsidiaries, while in the Philippines these numbers were 35 percent and 38 percent, respectively.

150. MNE=multinational enterprise.

151. See Williamson (1975) for the transactions cost approach to the theory of the firm.

152. The former builds on Holmström and Milgrom (1991), while the latter builds on Aghion and Tirole (1997).

153. The property rights approach with incomplete contracts was developed by Grossman and Hart (1986) and Hart and Moore (1990).

154. As the reader can imagine, this is too simplistic, yet it captures the essence of the basic approach to incomplete contracts.

155. The data cover the years 1987, 1989, 1992, and 1994.

156. I am grateful to Pol Antràs for providing the data for this figure, which essentially reproduces figure 2 in Antràs (2003).

157. Defever and Toubal (2010) report that a survey of French multinationals performed by the Service des Études Statistiques Industrielles found that these firms perceive the fixed cost of outsourcing to be higher than the fixed costs of vertical integration. I will discuss the French data later.

158. Yeaple (2006) uses the U.S. Bureau of Economic Analysis data, while Nunn and Trefler (2008) use data from the U.S. Census Bureau. The former data are confidential, while the latter are not.

159. Because at this level of disaggregation there is no data on R&D intensity, Nunn and Trefler consider skill intensity as an alternative proxy for headquarter intensity.

160. Using similar data for 1997, Bernard, Jensen, Redding and Schott (2010a) also report a positive correlation between a sector's capital intensity and its share of intrafirm imports. In addition, they find that this share is relatively higher for imports in capital-intensive sectors from capital-abundant countries. However, while they find that higher skill intensity raises the share of intrafirm imports, in line with Nunn and Trefler (2008), they also find that this share is higher for imports from more skill-scarce countries. In other words, while imports from more capital-abundant countries have a higher share of intrafirm trade, imports from skill-abundant countries have a lower share of intrafirm trade. This difference between capital and skill, which are usually considered to be complements in production, is puzzling, and no explanation is yet available.

161. This is also true for smaller firms, with fewer than 200 employees, who outsource relatively more than the larger firms both at home and abroad; see Kohler and Smolka (2009, table 2).

162. See Nocke and Yeaple (2006), Bernard, Redding, and Schott (2006), Feenstra and Ma (2008), Arkolakis and Muendler (2008), and Eckel and Neary (2010).

163. Unit values are calculated by dividing the value of exports by a quantity measure. The quantity can be a weight, such as kilos of steel, or it can be the number of units, such as television sets. In the latter example the unit value of televisions may reflect the average price, which depends on how many large- vs. small-screen sets are exported.

164. See Schott (2004), Hummels and Klenow (2005), and Hallak and Schott (2010).

165. Khandelwal (2010) uses a different methodology for estimating the quality of U.S. imports, which also accounts for horizontal product differentiation.

166. See, for example, Johnson (2010) and Manova and Zhang (2009).

167. See Helpman (2004) for a review.

168. See Helpman (2004, chapter 5).
169. See, however, Atkeson and Burstein (2010) for a recent exception.
170. See Costantini and Melitz (2008) and Bustos (2009) for attempts to examine this link. In more recent work in progress, Burstein and Melitz have identified interesting transitional dynamics that result from the interaction between firms' decisions to export and their decisions to invest in technology.

Bibliography

Abraham, Katharine G. and Susan K. Taylor. 1996. "Firms' Use of Outside Contractors: Theory and Evidence." *Journal of Labor Economics* 14: 394–424.

Acemoglu, Daron, Simon Johnson, and James Robinson. 2005. "The Rise of Europe: Atlantic Trade, Institutional Change, and Economic Growth." *American Economic Review* 95: 546–579.

Aghion, Philippe and Peter Howitt. 1992. "A Model of Growth through Creative Destruction." *Econometrica* 60: 323–351.

Aghion, Philippe and Jean Tirole. 1997. "Formal and Real Authority in Organizations." *Journal of Political Economy* 105: 1–29.

Alfaro, Laura and Andrew Charlton. 2009. "Intra-Industry Foreign Direct Investment." *American Economic Review* 99: 2096–2119.

Allen, Robert C. 2009. *The British Industrial Revolution in Global Perspective* (Cambridge, UK: Cambridge University Press).

Alvarez, Fernando and Robert E. Lucas, Jr. 2007. "General Equilibrium Analysis of the Eaton-Kortum Model of International Trade." *Journal of Monetary Economics* 54: 1726–1768.

Anderson, James and Eric van Wincoop. 2003. "Gravity with Gravitas: A Solution to the Border Puzzle." *American Economic Review* 93: 170–192.

Antràs, Pol. 2003. "Firms, Contracts, and Trade Structure." *Quarterly Journal of Economics* 118: 1375–1418.

Antràs, Pol and Elhanan Helpman. 2004. "Global Sourcing." *Journal of Political Economy* 112: 552–580.

Antràs, Pol and Elhanan Helpman. 2008. "Contractual Frictions and Global Sourcing." In Elhanan Helpman, Dalia Marin, and Thierry Verdier (eds.), *The Organization of Firms in a Global Economy* (Cambridge, MA: Harvard University Press).

Antweiler, Werner and Daniel Trefler. 2002. "Increasing Returns and All That: A View from Trade." *American Economic Review* 92: 93–119.

Arkolakis, Costas, Svetlana Demidova, Peter J. Klenow, and Andrés Rodríguez-Clare. 2008. "Endogenous Variety and the Gains from Trade." *American Economic Review* (Papers and Proceedings) 98: 444–450.

Arkolakis, Costas and Marc-Andreas Muendler. 2008. "The Extensive Margin of Exporting Goods: A Firm-Level Analysis." Mimeo.

Arrow, Kenneth J. and Frank H. Hahn. 1971. *General Competitive Analysis* (San Francisco: Holden-Day).

Atkeson, Andrew and Ariel Burstein. 2010. "Innovation, Firm Dynamics, and International Trade." *Journal of Political Economy* 118: 433–484.

Autor, David H., Lawrence F. Katz, and Melissa Schettini Kearney. 2008. "Trends in U.S. Wage Inequality: Re-assessing the Revisionists." *Review of Economics and Statistics* 90: 300–323.

Aw, Bee-Yan, Sukkyun Chung, and Mark J. Roberts. 2000. "Productivity and Turnover in the Export Market: Micro-level Evidence from the Republic of Korea and Taiwan (China)." *World Bank Economic Review* 14: 65–90.

Balassa, Bela. 1966. "Tariff Reductions and Trade in Manufactures among the Industrial Countries." *American Economic Review* 56: 466–473.

Balassa, Bela. 1967. *Trade Liberalization among Industrial Countries* (New York: McGraw-Hill).

Baldwin, John R. and Wulong Gu. 2003. "Export Market Participation and Productivity Performance in Canadian Manufacturing." *Canadian Journal of Economics* 36: 634–657.

Baldwin, Robert E. 1971. "Determinants of the Commodity Structure of U.S. Trade." *American Economic Review* 61: 126–146.

Balistreri, Edward J., Russel H. Hillberry, and Thomas F. Rutherford. 2008. "Structural Estimation and Solution of International Trade Models with Heterogeneous Firms." Working Paper 09/89, CER-ETH—Center of Economic Research at ETH Zurich.

Bardi, Edward J. and Michael Tracey. 1991. "Transportation Outsourcing: A Survey of U.S. Practices." *International Journal of Physical Distribution and Logistics Management* 21: 15–21.

Bartel, Ann, Saul Lach, and Nachum Sicherman. 2005. "Outsourcing and Technological Change." National Bureau of Economic Research (NBER) Working Paper No. 11158.

Bernard, Andrew B., Jonathan Eaton, J. Bradford Jensen, and Samuel Kortum. 2003. "Plants and Productivity in International Trade." *American Economic Review* 93: 1268–1290.

Bernard, Andrew B. and J. Bradford Jensen. 1995. "Exporters, Jobs, and Wages in U.S. Manufacturing, 1976–1987." *Brookings Papers on Economic Activity, Microeconomics* 67–119.

Bernard, Andrew B. and J. Bradford Jensen. 1999. "Exceptional Exporter Performance: Cause, Effect, or Both?" *Journal of International Economics* 47: 1–25.

Bernard, Andrew B. and J. Bradford Jensen. 2004. "Why Some Firms Export." *Review of Economics and Statistics* 86: 561–569.

Bernard, Andrew B., J. Bradford Jensen, Stephen J. Redding, and Peter K. Schott. 2007. "Firms in International Trade." *Journal of Economic Perspectives* 21: 105–130.

Bernard, Andrew B., J. Bradford Jensen, Stephen J. Redding, and Peter K. Schott. 2010a. "Intra-Firm Trade and Product Contractibility." *American Economic Review* (Papers and Proceedings) 100: 444–448.

Bernard, Andrew B., J. Bradford Jensen, Stephen J. Redding, and Peter K. Schott. 2010b. "Intra-Firm Trade and Product Contractibility (Long Version)." NBER Working Paper No. 15881.

Bernard, Andrew B., J. Bradford Jensen, and Peter K. Schott. 2009. "Importers, Exporters, and Multinationals: A Portrait of U.S. Firms that Trade Goods." In Timothy Dunne, J. Bradford Jensen, and Mark J. Roberts (eds.), *Producer Dynamics: New Evidence from Micro Data* (Chicago: University of Chicago Press).

Bernard, Andrew B., Stephen J. Redding, and Peter K. Schott. 2006. "Multi-Product Firms and Product Switching." NBER Working Paper No. 12782.

Bernard, Andrew B., Stephen J. Redding, and Pete K. Schott. 2007. "Comparative Advantage and Heterogeneous Firms." *Review of Economic Studies* 74: 31–66.

Bernard, Andrew B., Stephen J. Redding, and Pete K. Schott. 2010a. "Multi-Product Firms and Product Switching." *American Economic Review* 100: 70–97.

Bernard, Andrew B., Stephen J. Redding, and Pete K. Schott. 2010b. "Multi-Product Firms and Trade Liberalization." *Quarterly Journal of Economics*, forthcoming.

Bernhofen, Daniel M. and John C. Brown. 2004. "A Direct Test of the Theory of Comparative Advantage: The Case of Japan," *Journal of Political Economy* 112: 48–67.

Bernhofen, Daniel M. and John C. Brown. 2005. "An Empirical Assessment of the Comparative Advantage Gains from Trade: Evidence from Japan." *American Economic Review* 95: 208–225.

Berry, Steven, James Levinsohn and Ariel Pakes. 1995. "Automobile Prices in Market Equilibrium." *Econometrica* 63: 841–890.

Blanchard, Olivier J. and Pedro Portugal. 2001. "What Hides Behind an Unemployment Rate: Comparing Portuguese and US Unemployment." *American Economic Review* 91: 187–207.

Blanchard, Olivier J. and Justin Wolfers. 2000. "The Role of Shocks and Institutions in the Rise of European Unemployment: The Aggregate Evidence." *Economic Journal* 110: C1-C33.

Blonigen, Bruce A. 2005. "A Review of the Empirical Literature on FDI Determinants." *Atlantic Economic Journal* 33: 383–403.

Botero, Juan C., Simeon Djankov, Rafael La Porta, Florencio Lopez-de-Silanes, and Andrei Shleifer. 2004. "The Regulation of Labor." *Quarterly Journal of Economics* 119: 1339–1382.

Bowen, Harry P., Edward E. Leamer, and Leo Sveikauskas. 1987. "Multi-country, Multifactor Tests of the Factor Abundance Theory." *American Economic Review* 77: 791–809.

Brainard, Lael S. 1997. "An Empirical Assessment of Proximity-Concentration Tradeoff between Multinational Sales and Trade." *American Economic Review* 87: 520–544.

Brecher, Richard. 1974. "Minimum Wage Rates and the Pure Theory of International Trade." *Quarterly Journal of Economics* 88: 98–116.

Brecher, Richard A. and Ehsan U. Choudhri. 1982. "The Leontief Paradox, Continued." *Journal of Political Economy* 90: 264–267.

Broda, Christian and David E. Weinstein. 2006. "Globalization and the Gains from Variety." *Quarterly Journal of Economics* 121: 541–585.

Bustos, Paula. 2009. "Trade Liberalization, Exports and Technology Upgrading: Evidence on the Impact of MERCOSUR on Argentinean Firms." *American Economic Review*, forthcoming.

Campa, Jose and Linda S. Goldberg. 1997. "The Evolving External Orientation of Manufacturing Industries: Evidence from Four Countries." *Federal Reserve Bank of New York Economic Policy Review* 4: 79–99.

Carr, David, James Markusen, and Keith Maskus. 2001. "Estimating the Knowledge-Capital Model of the Multinational Enterprise." *American Economic Review* 91: 691–708.

Caves, Douglas W., Laurits R. Christensen, and Joseph A. Swanson. 1981. "Productivity Growth, Scale Economies, and Capacity Utilization in U.S. Railroads, 1955–74." *American Economic Review* 71: 994–1002.

Caves, Richard E. 2007. *Multinational Enterprise and Economic Analysis* (Cambridge, UK: Cambridge University Press, 3rd ed.).

Chamberlin, Edward H. 1933. *The Theory of Monopolistic Competition* (Cambridge, MA: Harvard University Press).

Chipman, John S. 1966. "A Survey of the Theory of International Trade: Part 3, the Modern Theory." *Econometrica* 34: 18–76.

Christensen, Laurits R. and William H. Greene. 1976. "Economies of Scale in U.S. Electric Power Generation." *Journal of Political Economy* 84: 655–676.

Cieślik, Andrzej. 2005. "Intraindustry Trade and Relative Factor Endowments." *Review of International Economics* 13: 904–926.

Clerides, Sofronis K., Saul Lach, and James R. Tybout. 1998. "Is Learning by Exporting Important? Micro-Dynamic Evidence from Colombia, Mexico, and Morocco." *Quarterly Journal of Economics* 113: 903–947.

Copeland, Brian. 1989. "Efficiency Wages in a Ricardian Model of International Trade." *Journal of International Economics* 27: 221–244.

Costantini, James A. and Marc Melitz. 2008. "The Dynamics of Firm-Level Adjustment to Trade Liberalization." In Elhanan Helpman, Dalia Marin, and Thierry Verdier (eds.), *The Organization of Firms in a Global Economy* (Cambridge, MA: Harvard University Press).

Costinot, Arnaud. 2009. "On the Origins of Comparative Advantage." *Journal of International Economics* 77: 255–264.

Council on Foreign Relations. 2002. *America—Still Unprepared, Still in Danger* (New York: Council on Foreign Relations).

Das, Mita, Mark Roberts, and James R. Tybout. 2007. "Market Entry Costs, Producer Heterogeneity and Export Dynamics." *Econometrica* 75: 837–873.

Davidson, Carl, Lawrence Martin, and Steven Matusz. 1999. "Trade and Search Generated Unemployment." *Journal of International Economics* 48: 271–299.

Davis, Donald R., David E. Weinstein, Scott C. Bradford, and Kazushige Shimpo. 1997. "Using International and Japanese Regional Data to Determine When the Factor Abundance Theory of Trade Works." *American Economic Review* 87: 421–446.

Davis, Donald R. and David E. Weinstein. 1999. "Economic Geography and Regional Production Structure: An Empirical Investigation." *European Economic Review* 43: 379–407.

Davis, Donald R. and David E. Weinstein. 2001. "An Account of Global Factor Trade." *American Economic Review* 91: 1423–1453.

Davis, Donald R. and David E. Weinstein. 2003. "Market Access, Economic Geography and Comparative Advantage: An Empirical Assessment." *Journal of International Economics* 59: 1–24.

Deardorff, Alan V. 1980. "The General Validity of the Law of Comparative Advantage." *Journal of Political Economy* 88: 941–957.

Debaere, Peter. 2005. "Monopolistic Competition and Trade Revisited: Testing the Model without Testing for Gravity." *Journal of International Economics* 66: 249–266.

Defever, Fabrice and Farid Toubal. 2010. "Productivity, Relation-Specific Inputs and the Sourcing Modes of Multinational Firms." Mimeo, January.

Delgado, Miguel A., Jose C. Fariñas, and Sonia Ruano. 2002. "Firm Productivity and Export Markets: A Non-Parametric Approach." *Journal of International Economics* 57: 397–422.

Diamond, Peter A. 1982a. "Demand Management in Search Equilibrium." *Journal of Political Economy* 90: 881–894.

Diamond, Peter A. 1982b. "Wage Determination and Efficiency in Search Equilibrium." *Review of Economic Studies* 49: 217–227.

Dixit, Avinash K. and Victor Norman. 1980. *Theory of International Trade* (Cambridge, UK: Cambridge University Press).

Dixit, Avinash K. and Victor Norman. 1986. "Gains from Trade without Lump-Sum Compensation." *Journal of International Economics* 21: 111–121.

Dixit, Avinash K. and Joseph E. Stiglitz. 1977. "Monopolistic Competition and Optimum Product Diversity." *American Economic Review* 67: 297–308.

Dollar, David and Edward N. Wolff. 1993. *Competitiveness, Convergence, and International Specialization* (Cambridge, MA: MIT Press).

Dornbusch, Rudiger, Stanley Fischer, and Paul A. Samuelson. 1977. "Comparative Advantage, Trade and Payments in a Ricardian Model with a Continuum of Goods." *American Economic Review* 67: 823–839.

Dornbusch, Rudiger, Stanley Fischer, and Paul A. Samuelson. 1980. "Heckscher-Ohlin Trade Theory with a Continuum of Goods." *Quarterly Journal of Economics* 95: 203–224.

Drelichman, Mauricio. 2005. "All that Glitters: Precious Metals, Rent Seeking, and the Decline of Spain." *European Review of Economic History* 9: 313–336.

Drelichman, Mauricio and Hans-Joachim Voth. 2008. "Institutions and the Resource Curse in Early Modern Spain." In Elhanan Helpman (ed.), *Institutions and Economic Performance* (Cambridge, MA: Harvard University Press).

Dunning, John H. 1977. "Trade, Location of Economic Activity and the MNE: A Search for an Eclectic Approach." In B. Ohlin, P.-O. Hesselborn, and P. M. Wijkman (eds.), *The International Allocation of Economic Activity: Proceedings of a Nobel Symposium Held at Stockholm* (London: Macmillan).

Dunning, John H. 1988. "The Eclectic Paradigm of International Business: A Restatement and Extensions." *Journal of International Business Studies* 19: 1–31.

Eaton, Jonathan and Samuel Kortum. 2002. "Technology, Geography, and Trade." *Econometrica* 70: 1741–1779.

Eaton, Jonathan, Samuel Kortum, and Francis Kramarz. 2004. "Dissecting Trade: Firms, Industries, and Export Destination." *American Economic Review* (Papers and Proceedings) 94: 150–154.

Eckel, Carsten and Peter J. Neary. 2010. "Multi-Product Firms and Flexible Manufacturing in the Global Economy." *Review of Economic Studies* 77: 188–217.

Ekholm, Karolina, Rikard Forslid, and James R. Markusen. 2007. "Export-Platform Foreign Direct Investment." *Journal of the European Economic Association* 5: 776–795.

Estevadeordal, Antoni, Brian Frantz, and Alan M. Taylor. 2003. "The Rise and Fall of World Trade: 1870–1939." *Quarterly Journal of Economics* 118: 359–407.

Ethier, Wilfred J. 1982a. "Decreasing Costs in International Trade and Frank Graham's Argument for Protection." *Econometrica* 50: 1243–1268.

Ethier, Wilfred J. 1982b. "National and International Returns to Scale in the Modern Theory of International Trade." *American Economic Review* 72: 389–405.

Ethier, Wilfred J. 1986. "The Multinational Firm." *Quarterly Journal of Economics* 101: 805–833.

Evenett, Simon J. and Wolfgang Keller. 2002. "On Theories Explaining the Success of the Gravity Equation." *Journal of Political Economy* 110: 281–316.

Fajgelbaum, Pablo, Gene M. Grossman, and Elhanan Helpman. 2009. "Income Distribution, Product Quality, and International Trade." NBER Working Paper No. 15329.

Feenstra, Robert C. 1994. "New Product Varieties and the Measurement of International Prices." *American Economic Review* 84: 157–177.

Feenstra, Robert C. 2009. "Measuring the Gains from Trade under Monopolistic Competition." Mimeo.

Feenstra, Robert C. and Gordon H. Hanson. 1996a. "Foreign Investment, Outsourcing and Relative Wages." In Robert C. Feenstra, Gene M. Grossman, and Douglas A. Irwin (eds.), *The Political Economy of Trade Policy* (Cambridge, MA: MIT Press).

Feenstra, Robert C. and Gordon H. Hanson. 1996b. "Globalization, Outsourcing, and Wage Inequality." *American Economic Review* (Papers and Proceedings) 86: 240–245.

Feenstra, Robert C. and Gordon H. Hanson. 1997. "Foreign Direct Investment and Relative Wages: Evidence from Mexico's Maquiladoras." *Journal of International Economics* 42: 371–393.

Feenstra, Robert C. and Hong Ma. 2008. "Optimal Choice of Product Scope for Multiproduct Firms." In Elhanan Helpman, Dalia Marin, and Thierry Verdier (eds.), *The Organization of Firms in a Global Economy* (Cambridge, MA: Harvard University Press).

Feenstra, Robert C. and David E. Weinstein. 2010. "Globalization, Markups, and the U.S. Price Level." NBER Working Paper No. 5749.

Findlay, Ronald and Kevin H. O'Rourke. 2007. *Power and Plenty: Trade, War, and the World Economy in the Second Millennium* (Princeton: Princeton University Press).

Fitzgerald, Doireann and Juan Carlos Hallak. 2004. "Specialization, Factor Accumulation and Development." *Journal of International Economics* 64: 277–302.

Flam, Harry and M. June Flanders. 1991. *Heckscher-Ohlin Trade Theory* (Cambridge, MA: MIT Press).

Ford, John L. 1982. "The Ricardian and Heckscher-Ohlin Explanations of Trade: A General Proof of an Equivalence Theorem and Its Implications." *Oxford Economic Papers* 34: 141–149.

Gardner, Elizabeth. 1991. "Going On Line with Outsiders." *Modern Healthcare* 21: 35–47.

Girma, Sourafel, Holger Görg, and Eric Strobl. 2004. "Exports, International Investment, and Plant Performance: Evidence from a Non-Parametric Test." *Economics Letters* 83: 317–324.

Girma, Sourafel, Richard Kneller, and Mauro Pisu. 2005. "Exports versus FDI: An Empirical Test." *Review of World Economics* 141: 193–218.

Goldberg, Pinelopi and Nina Pavcnik. 2007. "Distributional Effects of Globalization in Developing Countries." *Journal of Economic Literature* 45: 39–82.

Graham, Frank D. 1923. "Some Aspects of Protection Further Considered." *Quarterly Journal of Economics* 37: 199–227.

Graham, Frank D. 1948. *The Theory of International Values* (Princeton: Princeton University Press).

Grossman, Gene M. and Elhanan Helpman. 1991. *Innovation and Growth in the Global Economy* (Cambridge, MA: MIT Press).

Grossman, Gene M. and Elhanan Helpman. 1996. "Foreign Investment with Endogenous Protection." In Robert C. Feenstra, Gene M. Grossman, and Douglas A. Irwin (eds.), *The Political Economy of Trade Policy* (Cambridge, MA: MIT Press).

Grossman, Gene M. and Elhanan Helpman. 2002a. "Integration versus Outsourcing in Industry Equilibrium." *Quarterly Journal of Economics* 117: 85–120.

Grossman, Gene M. and Elhanan Helpman. 2002b. *Interest Groups and Trade Policy* (Princeton: Princeton University Press).

Grossman, Gene M. and Elhanan Helpman. 2004. "Managerial Incentives and the International Organization of Production." *Journal of International Economics* 63: 237–262.

Grossman, Gene M., Elhanan Helpman, and Adam Szeidl. 2006. "Optimal Integration Strategies for the Multinational Firm." *Journal of International Economics* 70: 216–238.

Grossman, Gene M. and Esteban Rossi-Hansberg. 2008. "Trading Tasks: A Simple Theory of Offshoring." *American Economic Review* 98: 1978–1997.

Grossman, Gene M. and Esteban Rossi-Hansberg. 2010. "External Economies and International Trade Redux." *Quarterly Journal of Economics* 125: 829–858.

Grossman, Sanford J. and Oliver D. Hart. 1986. "The Costs and Benefits of Ownership: A Theory of Vertical and Lateral Integration." *Journal of Political Economy* 94: 691–719.

Grubel, Herbert G. and Peter J. Lloyd. 1975. *Intra-Industry Trade: The Theory and Measurement of International Trade in Differentiated Products* (London: Macmillan).

Hakura, Dalia S. 2001. "Why Does HOV Fail? The Role of Technological Differences within the EC." *Journal of International Economics* 54: 361–382.

Hallak, Juan Carlos. 2006. "Product Quality and the Direction of Trade." *Journal of International Economics* 68: 238–265.

Hallak, Juan Carlos and Peter K. Schott. 2010. "Estimating Cross-Country Differences in Product Quality." *Quarterly Journal of Economics*, forthcoming.

Hanson, Gordon H. and Chong Xiang. 2004. "The Home-Market Effect and Bilateral Trade Patterns." *American Economic Review* 94: 1108–1129.

Hanson, Gordon H., Raymond J. Mataloni, Jr., and Matthew J. Slaughter. 2001. "Expansion Strategies of U.S. Multinational Firms." In Dani Rodrik and Susan Collins (eds.), *Brookings Trade Forum 2001* (Washington, DC: Brookings Institution).

Hanson, Gordon H., Raymond J. Mataloni, Jr., and Matthew J. Slaughter. 2005. "Vertical Production Networks in Multinational Firms." *Review of Economics and Statistics* 87: 664–678.

Harrigan, James. 1995. "Factor Endowments and the International Location of Production: Econometric Evidence for the OECD, 1970–1985." *Journal of International Economics* 39: 123–141.

Hart, Oliver D. and John Moore. 1990. "Property Rights and the Nature of the Firm." *Journal of Political Economy* 98: 1119–1158.

Head, Keith and John Ries. 2001. "Increasing Returns versus National Product Differentiation as an Explanation for the Pattern of US-Canada Trade." *American Economic Review* 91: 858–876.

Head, Keith and John Ries. 2003. "Heterogeneity and the FDI versus Export Decision of Japanese Manufacturers." *Journal of the Japanese and International Economy* 17: 448–467.

Heckscher, Eli F. 1919. "The Effect of Foreign Trade on the Distribution of Income." In Harry Flam and M. June Flanders, *Heckscher-Ohlin Trade Theory* (Cambridge, MA: MIT Press, 2001).

Helper, Susan. 1991. "Strategy and Irreversibility in Supplier Relations: The Case of the U.S. Automobile Industry." *Business History Review* 65: 781–824.

Helpman, Elhanan. 1976. "Solutions of General Equilibrium Problems for a Trading World." *Econometrica* 44: 547–559.

Helpman, Elhanan. 1981. "International Trade in the Presence of Product Differentiation, Economies of Scale and Monopolistic Competition: A Chamberlin-Hechscher-Ohlin Approach." *Journal of International Economics* 11: 305–340.

Helpman, Elhanan. 1984. "A Simple Theory of International Trade with Multinational Corporations." *Journal of Political Economy* 92: 451–471.

Helpman, Elhanan. 1987. "Imperfect Competition and International Trade: Evidence from Fourteen Industrial Countries." *Journal of the Japanese and International Economies* 1: 62–81.

Helpman, Elhanan. 2004. *The Mystery of Economic Growth* (Cambridge, MA: Belknap Press of Harvard University Press).

Helpman, Elhanan and Oleg Itskhoki. 2010. "Labor Market Rigidities, Trade and Unemployment." *Review of Economic Studies* 77: 1100–1137.

Helpman, Elhanan, Oleg Itskhoki, and Stephen J. Redding. 2010a. "Inequality and Unemployment in a Global Economy." *Econometrica* 78: 1239–1283.

Helpman, Elhanan, Oleg Itskhoki, and Stephen J. Redding. 2010b. "Unequal Effects of Trade on Workers with Different Abilities." *Journal of the European Economic Association* (Papers and Proceedings) 8 (2–3): 421–433.

Helpman, Elhanan and Paul R. Krugman. 1985. *Market Structure and Foreign Trade* (Cambridge, MA: MIT Press).

Helpman, Elhanan, Marc J. Melitz, and Yona Rubinstein. 2008. "Trading Partners and Trading Volumes." *Quarterly Journal of Economics* 123: 441–487.

Helpman, Elhanan, Marc J. Melitz, and Stephen R. Yeaple. 2004. "Export versus FDI with Heterogeneous Firms." *American Economic Review* 94: 300–316.

Holmström, Bengt and Paul Milgrom. 1991. "Multitask Principal-Agent Analyses: Incentive Contracts, Asset Ownership, and Job Design." *Journal of Law, Economics and Organization* 7: 24–52.

Huber, J. Richard. 1971. "Effect on Prices of Japan's Entry into World Commerce after 1858." *Journal of Political Economy* 79: 614–628.

Hummels, David, Jun Ishii, and Kei-Mu Yi. 2001. "The Nature and Growth of Vertical Specialization in World Trade." *Journal of International Economics* 54: 75–96.

Hummels, David and Peter J. Klenow. 2005. "The Variety and Quality of a Nation's Exports." *American Economic Review* 95: 704–723.

Hummels, David and James Levinsohn. 1995. "Monopolistic Competition and International Trade: Reconsidering the Evidence." *Quarterly Journal of Economics* 110: 799–836.

Hunter, Linda. 1991. "The Contribution of Non-Homothetic Preferences to Trade." *Journal of International Economics* 30: 345–358.

Irwin, Douglas A. 2005. "The Welfare Costs of Autarky: Evidence from the Jeffersonian Embargo, 1807–1809." *Review of International Economics* 13: 631–645.

Johnson, Robert. 2010. "Trade and Prices with Heterogeneous Firms." Mimeo.

Jones, Ronald W. 1965. "The Structure of Simple General Equilibrium Models." *Journal of Political Economy* 73: 557–572.

Jones, Ronald W. 1971. "A Three-Factor Model in Theory, Trade and History." In Jagdish N. Bhagwati, Ronald W. Jones, Robert A. Mundell, and Jaroslav Vanek (eds.), *Trade, Balance of Payments and Growth: Papers in International Economics in Honor of Charles P. Kindleberger* (Amsterdam: North-Holland): 3–21.

Jones, Ronald W. 1980. "Comparative and Absolute Advantage." *Schweizerische Zeitschrift für Volkswirtschaft und Statistik* 3: 235–260.

Jones, Ronald W. and Jose A. Scheinkman. 1977. "The Relevance of the Two-Sector Production Model in Trade Theory." *Journal of Political Economy* 85: 909–935.

Juhn, Chinhui, Kevin M. Murphy, and Robert H. Topel. 1991. "Why Has the Natural Rate of Unemployment Increased over Time?" *Brookings Papers on Economic Activity* 2: 75–142.

Kemp, Murray C. 1962. "The Gains from International Trade." *Economic Journal* 72: 803–819.

Khandelwal, Amit. 2010. "The Long and Short (of) Quality Ladders." *Review of Economic Studies* 77: 1450–1476.

Knight, Frank H. 1924. "Some Fallacies in the Interpretation of Social Costs." *Quarterly Journal of Economics* 38: 582–606.

Kohler, Wilhelm K. and Marcel Smolka. 2009. "Global Sourcing Decisions and Firm Productivity: Evidence from Spain." CESifo Working Paper No. 2903.

Krugman, Paul R. 1979. "Increasing Returns, Monopolistic Competition, and International Trade." *Journal of International Economics* 9: 469–479.

Krugman, Paul R. 1980. "Scale Economies, Product Differentiation, and the Pattern of Trade." *American Economic Review* 70: 950–959.

Krugman, Paul R. 1981. "Intraindustry Specialization and the Gains from Trade." *Journal of Political Economy* 89: 959–973.

Krugman, Paul R. and Maurice Obstfeld. 2009. *International Economics: Theory and Policy*, 8th ed. (Boston: Pearson, Addison Wesley).

Lancaster, Kelvin. 1979. *Variety, Equity, and Efficiency* (New York: Columbia University Press).

Lancaster, Kelvin. 1980. "Intra-Industry Trade under Perfectly Monopolistic Competition." *Journal of International Economics* 10: 151–175.

Leamer, Edward E. 1980. "The Leontief Paradox, Reconsidered." *Journal of Political Economy* 88: 495–503.

Leamer, Edward E. 1984. *Sources of International Comparative Advantage* (Cambridge, MA: MIT Press).

Leamer, Edward E. and James Levinsohn. 1995. "International Trade Theory: The Evidence." In Gene M. Grossman and Kenneth S. Rogoff (eds.), *Handbook of International Economics*, vol. 3 (New York: Elsevier Science).

Lemieux, Thomas. 2006. "Increasing Residual Wage Inequality: Composition Effects, Noisy Data or Rising Skill Returns?" *American Economic Review* 96: 461–498.

Leontief, Wassily. 1953. "Domestic Production and Foreign Trade: The American Capital Position Re-Examined." *Proceedings of the American Philosophical Society* 97: 332–349.

Levchenko, Andrei. 2007. "Institutional Quality and International Trade." *Review of Economic Studies* 74: 791–819.

McCormick, Michael. 2001. *Origins of the European Economy: Communications and Commerce, AD 300–900* (New York: Cambridge University Press).

McDougall, G. D. A. 1951. "British and American Exports: A Study Suggested by the Theory of Comparative Costs, Part 1." *Economic Journal* 61: 697–724.

McDougall, G. D. A. 1952. "British and American Exports: A Study Suggested by the Theory of Comparative Costs, Part 2." *Economic Journal* 62: 487–521.

McKenzie, Lionel W. 1953–1954. "Specialization and Efficiency in World Production." *Review of Economic Studies* 21: 165–180.

McKenzie, Lionel W. 1954. "On Equilibrium in Graham's Model of World Trade and Other Competitive Systems." *Econometrica* 22: 147–161.

Manova, Kalina and Zhiwei Zhang. 2009. "Quality Heterogeneity across Firms and Export Destinations." Mimeo.

Marin, Dalia and Thierry Verdier. 2008a. "Competing in Organizations: Firm Heterogeneity and International Trade." In Elhanan Helpman, Dalia Marin, and Thierry Verdier (eds.), *The Organization of Firms in a Global Economy* (Cambridge, MA: Harvard University Press).

Marin, Dalia and Thierry Verdier. 2008b. "Power Inside the Firm and the Market: A General Equilibrium Approach." *Journal of the European Economic Association* 6: 758–788.

Markusen, James R. 1984. "Multinationals, Multi-Plant Economies and the Gain from Trade." *Journal of International Economics* 16: 205–216.

Markusen, James R. 2002. *Multinational Firms and the Theory of International Trade* (Cambridge, MA: MIT Press).

Marshall, Alfred. 1920. *Principles of Economics*, 8th ed. (London: Macmillan).

Matsuyama, Kiminori. 2007. "Beyond Icebergs: Towards a Theory of Biased Globalization." *Review of Economic Studies* 74: 237–253.

Matusz, Steven J. 1986. "Implicit Contracts, Unemployment and International Trade." *Economic Journal* 96: 71–84.

Mayda, Anna Maria and Dani Rodrik. 2005. "Why Are Some People (and Countries) More Protectionist Than Others?" *European Economic Review* 49: 1393–1691.

Melitz, Marc J. 2003. "The Impact of Trade on Intra-Industry Reallocations and Aggregate Industry Productivity." *Econometrica* 71: 1695–1725.

Melitz, Marc J. and Gianmarco Ottaviano. 2008. "Market Size, Trade, and Productivity." *Review of Economic Studies* 75: 295–316.

Mill, John Stuart. 1909. *Principles of Political Economy* (London: Longmans, Green) (original ed., 1848).

Mortensen, Dale T. and Christopher A. Pissarides. 1994. "Job Creation and Job Destruction in the Theory of Unemployment." *Review of Economic Studies* 61: 397–415.

Mussa, Michael. 1974. "Tariffs and the Distribution of Income: The Importance of Factor Specificity, Substitutability, and Intensity in the Short and Long Run." *Journal of Political Economy* 82: 1191–1204.

Neary, J. Peter. 1978. "Short-Run Capital Specificity and the Pure Theory of International Trade." *Economic Journal* 88: 488–510.

Nickell, Steven, Luca Nunziata, Wolfgang Ochel, and Glenda Quintini. 2002. "The Beveridge Curve, Unemployment and Wages in the OECD from the 1960s to the 1990s." CEP Discussion Paper, London School of Economics Centre for Economic Performance.

Nocke, Volker and Stephen R. Yeaple. 2006. "Globalization and Endogenous Firm Scope." NBER Working Paper No. 12322.

North, Douglas C. and Barry R. Weingast. 1989. "Constitutions and Commitment: Evolution of Institutions Governing Public Choice in Seventeenth Century England." *Journal of Economic History* 49: 803–832.

Nunn, Nathan. 2007. "Relationship-Specificity, Incomplete Contracts, and the Pattern of Trade." *Quarterly Journal of Economics* 132: 569–600.

Nunn, Nathan and Daniel Trefler. 2008. "The Boundaries of the Multinational Firm: An Empirical Analysis." In Elhanan Helpman, Dalia Marin, and Thierry Verdier (eds.), *The Organization of Firms in a Global Economy* (Cambridge, MA: Harvard University Press).

Obstfeld, Maurice and Alan M. Taylor. 2004. *Global Capital Markets: Integration, Crisis, and Growth* (New York: Cambridge University Press).

Ohlin, Bertil. 1924. "The Theory of Trade." In Harry Flam and M. June Flanders, *Heckscher-Ohlin Trade Theory* (Cambridge, MA: MIT Press, 2001).

Ohlin, Bertil. 1933. *Interregional and International Trade* (Cambridge, MA: Harvard University Press).

Ohyama, Michihiro. 1972. "Trade and Welfare in General Equilibrium." *Keio Economic Studies* 9: 37–73.

Oi, Walter Y. and T. L. Idson. 1999. "Firm Size and Wages." In Orly Ashenfelter and David Card (eds.), *Handbook of Labor Economics,* vol. 3 (Amsterdam: Elsevier).

Organization for Economic Cooperation and Development. 2002. *OECD Economic Outlook 71* (Paris: OECD).

O'Rourke, Kevin H. and Richard Sinnott. 2001. "What Determines Attitudes Towards Protection? Some Cross-Country Evidence." In Susan M. Collins and Dani Rodrik (eds.), *Brookings Trade Forum 2001* (Washington, DC: Brookings Institute Press).

O'Rourke, Kevin H. and Jeffrey G. Williamson. 1999. *Globalization and History: The Evolution of the Nineteenth-Century Atlantic Economy* (Cambridge, MA: MIT Press).

O'Rourke, Kevin H. and Jeffrey G. Williamson. 2002. "When Did Globalization Begin?" *European Review of Economic History* 6: 23–50.

Pavcnik, Nina. 2002. "Trade Liberalization, Exit, and Productivity Improvements: Evidence from Chilean Plants." *Review of Economic Studies* 69: 245–276.

Pissarides, Christopher A. 2000. *Equilibrium Unemployment Theory* (Cambridge, MA: MIT Press, 2nd ed.).

Pomeranz, Kenneth. 2000. *The Great Divergence: China, Europe, and the Making of the Modern World Economy* (Princeton: Princeton University Press).

Porter, Michael E. 1990. *The Competitive Advantage of Nations* (New York: Free Press).

Rajan, Raghuram and Julie Wulf. 2006. "The Flattening Firm: Evidence from Panel Data on the Changing Nature of Corporate Hierarchies." *Review of Economics and Statistics* 88: 759–773.

Reeve, Trevor A. 2006. "Factor Endowments and Industrial Structure." *Review of International Economics* 14: 30–53.

Ricardo, David. 1971. *On the Principles of Political Economy, and Taxation* (Harmondsworth: Pelican Books [text, 3rd ed., 1821; original ed., 1817]).

Roberts, Mark J. and James R. Tybout. 1997. "The Decision to Export in Colombia: An Empirical Model of Entry with Sunk Costs." *American Economic Review* 87: 545–564.

Romalis, John. 2004. "Factor Proportions and the Structure of Commodity Trade." *American Economic Review* 94: 67–97.

Rybczynski, Tadeusz N. 1955. "Factor Endowments and Relative Commodity Prices." *Economica* 22: 336–341.

Samuelson, Paul A. 1939. "The Gains from International Trade." *Canadian Journal of Economics and Political Science* 5: 195–205.

Samuelson, Paul A. 1948. "International Trade and the Equalization of Factor Prices." *Economic Journal* 58: 163–184.

Samuelson, Paul A. 1954. "Transfer Problem and Transport Cost, II: Analysis of Effects of Trade Impediments." *Economic Journal* 64: 264–289.

Samuelson, Paul A. 1962. "The Gains from International Trade Once Again." *Economic Journal* 72: 820–829.

Scheve, Kenneth F. and Matthew J. Slaughter. 2001. "What Determines Individual Trade-Policy Preferences?" *Journal of International Economics* 54: 267–292.

Schott, Peter K. 2004. "Across-Product versus Within-Product Specialization in International Trade." *Quarterly Journal of Economics* 119: 647–678.

Sheu, Gloria Yah-Shing. 2010. "Product Differentiation and Firm Heterogeneity in International Trade." Ph.D. thesis, Harvard University.

Shimer, Robert. 2005. "The Cyclical Behavior of Equilibrium Unemployment and Vacancies." *American Economic Review* 95: 25–49.

Smith, Adam. 1937. *The Wealth of Nations* (New York: Modern Library [original ed., 1776]).

Stern, Robert M. 1962. "British and American Productivity and Comparative Costs in International Trade." *Oxford Economic Papers* 14: 275–296.

Stole, Lars A. and Jeffrey Zwiebel. 1996a. "Intra-Firm Bargaining under Non-Binding Contracts." *Review of Economic Studies* 63: 375–410.

Stole, Lars A. and Jeffrey Zwiebel. 1996b. "Organizational Design and Technology Choice under Intrafirm Bargaining." *American Economic Review* 86: 195–222.

Stolper, Wolfgang W. and Paul A. Samuelson. 1941. "Protection and Real Wages." *Review of Economic Studies* 9: 58–73.

Tinbergen, Jan. 1962. *Shaping the World Economy* (New York: Twentieth Century Fund).

Tomiura, Eiichi. 2007. "Foreign Outsourcing, Exporting, and FDI: A Productivity Comparison at the Firm Level." *Journal of International Economics* 72: 113–127.

Trefler, Daniel. 1993. "International Factor Price Differences: Leontief Was Right!" *Journal of Political Economy* 101: 961–987.

Trefler, Daniel. 1995. "The Case of the Missing Trade and Other Mysteries." *American Economic Review* 85: 1029–1046.

Trefler, Daniel. 2004. "The Long and Short of the Canada-U.S. Free Trade Agreement." *American Economic Review* 94: 870–895.

Tybout, James R. and M. Daniel Westbrook. 1995. "Trade Liberalization and the Dimensions of Efficiency Changes in Mexican Manufacturing Industries." *Journal of International Economics* 39: 53–78.

UNCTAD. 1998. *World Investment Report: Trends and Determinants* (New York and Geneva: United Nations Conference on Trade and Development).

UNCTAD. 2004. *World Investment Report: The Shift Towards Services* (New York and Geneva: United Nations Conference on Trade and Development).

UNCTAD. 2008. *World Investment Report: Transnational Corporations and the Infrastructure Challenge* (New York and Geneva: United Nations Conference on Trade and Development).

UNCTAD. 2009. *World Investment Report: Transnational Corporations, Agricultural Production and Development* (New York and Geneva: United Nations Conference on Trade and Development).

Vanek, Jaroslav. 1968. "The Factor Proportions Theory: The N-Factor Case." *Kyklos* 21: 749–754.

Verhoogen, Eric. 2008. "Trade, Quality Upgrading, and Wage Inequality in the Mexican Manufacturing Sector: Theory and Evidence from an Exchange Rate Shock." *Quarterly Journal of Economics* 123: 489–530.

Viner, Jacob. 1965. *Studies in the Theory of International Trade* (New York: Harper and Brothers [original ed., 1937]).

de Vries, Jan. 1993. "Between Purchasing Power and the World of Goods: Understanding the Household Economy in Early Modern Europe." In John Brewer and Roy Porter (eds.), *Consumption and the World of Goods* (London: Routledge).

Wake, C. H. H. 1986. "The Volume of European Spice Imports at the Beginning and End of the Fifteenth Century." *Journal of European Economic History* 15: 621–635.

Ward-Perkins, Bryan. 2005. *The Fall of Rome and the End of Civilization* (Oxford: Oxford University Press).

Williamson, Oliver E. 1975. *Markets and Hierarchies: Analysis and Antitrust Implications* (New York: Free Press).

Wilson, Charles A. 1980. "On the General Structure of Ricardian Models with a Continuum of Goods: Applications to Growth, Tariff Theory, and Technical Change." *Econometrica* 48: 1675–1702.

World Trade Organization. 2006. *International Trade Statistics 2006* (Geneva: World Trade Organization).

World Trade Organization. 2008. *World Trade Report 2008: Transnational Corporations, and the Infrastructure Challenge* (Geneva: World Trade Organization).

Yeaple, Stephen R. 2003a. "The Complex Integration Strategies of Multinationals and Cross Country Dependencies in the Structure of Foreign Direct Investment." *Journal of International Economics* 60: 293–314.

Yeaple, Stephen R. 2003b. "The Role of Skill Endowments in the Structure of U.S. Outward Foreign Direct Investment." *Review of Economics and Statistics* 85: 726–734.

Yeaple, Stephen R. 2006. "Offshoring, Foreign Direct Investment, and the Structure of U.S. Trade." *Journal of the European Economic Association* (Papers and Proceedings) 4: 602–611.

Yeaple, Stephen R. 2009. "Firm Heterogeneity and the Structure of U.S. Multinational Activity." *Journal of International Economics* 78: 206–215.

Yeats, Alexander J. 2001. "Just How Big Is Global Production Sharing?" In Sven W. Arndt and Henryk Kierzkowski (eds.), *Fragmentation: New Production Patterns in the World Economy* (Oxford: Oxford University Press).

Yi, Kei-Mu. 2003. "Can Vertical Specialization Explain the Growth of World Trade?" *Journal of Political Economy* 111: 52–102.

Zhu, Susan Chun and Daniel Trefler. 2005. "Trade and Inequality in Developing Countries: A General Equilibrium Analysis." *Journal of International Economics* 65: 21–48.

Index